The
Drums of ECK

The
Drums of ECK

Paul Twitchell

ECKANKAR
Minneapolis, MN

The Drums of ECK

Printed in U.S.A.
ISBN: 0-914766-04-x

Cover illustration by Gary Cooper
Cover design by Lois Stanfield

Dedicated to

Gail

Foreword

The narrative which is laid down in this book, The Drums of ECK, may appear to the reader to be fiction but it is a true story. It is taken from my personal memories of what happened during the stirring times of the American-Mexican War which was fought in the years 1846–48, principally on the soil of old Mexico.

I was there so everything is recorded as accurately as my memory allows. Occasionally, I checked back on certain events to re-check my memory through the ECK-Vidya, a method used by the ECKANKAR Masters to look at the past lives. The characters who appear in this story, including myself as Peddar Zaskq, which is my real name, were actual people living in those times.

The names we know from history including General Winfield Scott, U.S. Grant, Robert E. Lee, Jefferson Davis, General Zachary Taylor, Jackson, Sherman and others which appear in this story actually served in their relative capacity and became prominent in the American Civil War.

The story is about the times I spent in Mexico during the years when James K. Polk, 11th president of the United States, was enchanted with its expansion—known to history as the Manifest Destiny.

The book itself is the unfolding of events, behind the facts of recorded history, of the daily lives of those who served in the little American army in its campaign across the vast lands of the unfortunate country of Mexico. It shows that man seldom learns his lesson of the past, for today history repeats itself with a different face and again we fight on a foreign soil, hoping to win for a government which will be sympathetic to our democratic form of rule.

Today, we have armies stationed in other parts of the world and fighting in foreign lands. All of which is a parallel with other eras of our history, especially that of our participation in the war with Mexico in 1846–48.

However, I write this story mostly to show the secret influence and the part the ECK force (the Cosmic life current) played—as always—during all times in history since the beginning of this world.

The events are exactly as they happened in those days when the American army invaded Mexico under General Zachary Taylor, who later became president of the United States. He was relieved of command by General Scott whose strategy won him fame in the annals of human history.

It was an era of brilliant men, but a time when war was so unpopular it created draft dodgers, riots and heavy taxes which the American public rebelled against. It also brought about the famous civil disobedience acts of Henry Thoreau who probably became the first to denounce an American war by refusing to report for duty. He set the style of revolt for our modern times.

Congress, as well as the public, fought James Polk to stop the war and the expansion. Politics became so dirty and muddled that he left his office at the end of his presidential term almost in disgrace, cancelling any ambition to run for another term.

The characters lived and breathed as people. I performed a small part during these times as the messenger of the SUGMAD. I was but in training for the Mastership, under the divine guidance of Rebazar Tarzs, who was then the MAHANTA, and Living ECK Master.

Paul Twitchell
London, England, 1969

2

Chapter One

T he sun was a torrid disk in the clear azure sky and the lonely world with its aged purple mountains loomed mysteriously against the hazy Mexican horizon on this sultry day of March 26, 1846.

High above the sunbaked world a Mexican eagle glided curiously watching the tiny American army crawling across the scorched prairie between the Nueces and Rio Grande rivers. With a wild hissing it dove toward the blue serpentine line to investigate the invaders of its domain.

There was little the king of the sky could do, for this invasion of Mexico was written upon the karmic scrolls of destiny. Even the politicians of the day recognized the significance of the events and made popular the phrase "Manifest Destiny". The United States was suffering pains of growth and had cast avaricious eyes toward the countries of Oregon, California and the Southwest.

William K. Polk rode into presidency on promises to annex California and the Southwest territory. He was determined to fight this war despite the opposition of the northern abolitionists who believed it was another excuse to add territory to the southern democratic slave block, and Mexico who resented the United States' intrusion upon her Texas neighbor.

The army was alerted for war when the Texas convention met at Austin, July 4, 1845 to vote on joining the Union.

3

The Eleventh Regiment received orders to move from Fort Dearborn to New Orleans. From there to Corpus Christi to join General Zachary Taylor's army swelling it to a force of six thousand troops, the largest assembled on American soil since the Revolutionary days.

In early March 1846, Polk ordered the army into the disputed territory to bivouac on the Rio Grande, opposite Matamoros, and establish by the right of force the American claim to the boundary lines.

Lieutenant Jed Blake, USA, Chief of Scouts for the Eleventh, riding at the head of his patrol, watched the eagle soar through the sky. He was hot, tired and worried. Some ominous shadow was stirring in his mind like impressions of the impending circumstances yet to come. Nothing seemed right in this brooding, mysterious land where the ancient gods watched over their own.

His horse shied away from a cactus thorn but Blake jerked it back on the trail again. He straightened his lanky, whip-rod body in the saddle and stared ahead with bright, yellow eyes set deep in a gaunt, narrow face. His mouth was pulled in a thin line, reflecting the depth of soul suffering.

He was a man in his middle twenties, untouched by nature in this hot, harsh land where the blowing sand turned the color of his blue uniform to a dusty gray. His ugly, flat-topped cap with its pinched bill was hardly enough to keep the boiling sun off his bronzed cheeks. He poured water from his canteen over a handkerchief and hung it under his cap, dropping it over the back of his neck.

His searching glance saw the vast flat sea of the prairie which caught the gleaming sunlight in the thick grass and threw off prisms of dancing colors. Heat shimmered in the thirsty waves across the tall, bayonet cactus that pushed thick heads high with patches of white blossoms — tiny beacons to guard against the gringo invasion.

This severe brooding world bothered Blake. He thought of what Peddar Zaskq, that strange man who was acting as a

4

scout for Blake's patrol, said about ECKANKAR, the Ancient Science of Soul Travel. But the smothering heat and weariness of the long march intensified his distress over the death of his younger brother in a recent Mexican ambush. He was, at least he felt so, neither a mystic nor a sensitive, so recognition of what he was to face was lacking.

The unnatural silence of this world was broken only by the thump of marching feet against the earth. It was a strange silence, pregnant with some dark meaning yet to be revealed. Into his consciousness came another sound and the Yankee army was a thin, blue serpent weaving its way across the sun-baked earth in rhythm to a strange roll of drums.

His glance toward the drummers brought a mild surprise for none were beating the march. He concluded that the heat was affecting his mind, and briefly watched the soaring eagle until his attention was drawn to Sergeant McQuillen who wheeled out of formation.

The Sergeant slowed his mount to a walk behind Blake and moved alongside of Private Campbell. Leaning across the saddle pommel he started talking in a moderate voice.

Blake's eyes narrowed. He let his glance slide along the column of riders. He wondered at McQuillen's continued campaign for an officer's commission which seemed to intensify after three years of effort. There was nothing unusual about these hard faced riders. They were dirty, superstitious, unwashed troopers who had no belief in God. They would start a fight as soon as repel an attack.

They were nothing but adventurers, troublemakers and looters, who had entered this mysterious land of the ancient gods. With the exception of a few, all had left their homes for gold, liquor and lust in this exotic land where the SUGMAD, the deity of that strange religion called ECKANKAR, would await ITS retribution for being aroused from a deep slumber over the centuries.

5

They expected to return as heroes but some of them would be left in the hot sands of the Mexican deserts, or the highlands, for the vultures and wolves to feed upon. Very few would return, but those who did would have empty hands and heavy hearts.

The heat dulled his brain and closing his eyes he half-listened to the thud of hooves against the hot sands. Something strange was going on around him. Opening his eyes again he quickly searched the landscape seeing nothing except the tough troopers who, after days on the march without the comforts of life, broke the silence occasionally with a ribald song.

A whisper and hoarse laughter from behind stung his ears and dug deeply into him. Suddenly he caught the impact of the words. The implication whipped him into action. Wheeling in the saddle, he saw McQuillen straightening up with a guilty expression on his heavy, scarred countenance.

Blake struggled against the rage that tried to sweep every particle of reason out of his brain. Suddenly it broke through his thin crust of control and added to the torture of the blazing sun and barren wastes.

He called, "Take over, Corporal Arnold. Fall out, McQuillen, and follow me!"

He whirled his horse off the trail into the deep sand leading the way recklessly through the thorny, blossoming cactus. Just beyond the first knoll he pulled up and whirled impatiently to the big sergeant, wondering how to discipline him.

McQuillen halted his mount. His flat face wore a patient, unassuming expression and his eyes held a steady glow like that of a trapped animal, unafraid, yet ready to defend itself with every possible wile.

Blake snapped an order for the sergeant to dismount, while at the same time slid off his horse. He was aware of his duty to the men who served under him but this situation warranted measures beyond regulations.

He wondered if an explanation about those rumors would serve any purpose. He was not responsible for his brother being elected to take charge of that ill-fated patrol. Some of the scouts saw him leaving the regimental headquarter's tent shortly before Henry was called and presumed Blake had talked the colonel into it.

Blake got wind of the order, protested it, and had volunteered for the duty, but was told that he was needed for a more important job. The right flank of the army needed all the protection it could get on its first leg to Matamoros.

This was an awkward moment. He took a deep breath and plunged into the midst of his troubles. "You were talking to Campbell about me!" he said bluntly.

McQuillen said smoothly, "I don't know what you mean, sir!"

A flush stained Blake's face as he studied the sergeant. McQuillen wore an ugly knife scar on his right cheek which slashed across a stubbled chin to his temple. His neck was a powerful corded column supported by heavy sloping shoulders and a thick tapered body. There was a drive which thrust out from him, a vitality and a strength that had in it the capacity of quick insistence and need. He was a big, tough soldier and an iron-hard man, well-spoken when he chose to be, but Blake knew him to be ambitious, selfish and self-controlled.

"You were talking about Henry's patrol. I asked that it not be discussed among the scouts," Blake said controlling his temper. "You take the graveyard watch for three nights."

McQuillen's right eyebrow raised slightly. He expected something but not this. The graveyard watch was rugged for one night, with its weird sounds and creepy shadows which the men often complained about, saying witches were about. But he was man enough to take anything the Lieutenant had to dish out.

7

"The graveyard watch for three nights?" he exclaimed in mock surprise. "For what? Because I made a little joke with Campbell?"

"The joke wasn't funny, Sergeant. You were telling Campbell that I got the Colonel to give that patrol to Henry for personal reasons!"

"You didn't hear right, Lieutenant," McQuillen said, his face impassive and controlled but his upper lip curled slightly.

Blake's self-control gave way. Impetuously he drove his fist into the sergeant's stubbled jaw. McQuillen sat down heavily in the hot sand rubbing his cheek with a hurt expression.

"What's that for?" he demanded in a voice quivering with rage, but deep within him was a growing satisfaction.

"For shooting off your mouth again, McQuillen. I warned you against it." Blake felt a deep rolling thunder of drums again in his head. He stopped for it was apparent that McQuillen had deliberately framed him. He had been a fool. He shook his head vigorously to clear it of those thundering drums.

The sergeant's face was a mask of hatred. He rose to one knee with both fists doubled, but stopped as hooves beating rapidly against the sand beyond the knoll were heard. Private Campbell rode into view and pulled up on the rise above them. Sitting sloppily astride his mount he stared bug-eyed at the sergeant who was rubbing a red welt on his cheekbone.

Blake snapped, "What is it, Campbell?"

He was aware that within minutes word would spread like wildfire among the troops that Blake had struck his noncom. McQuillen had played his cards right, for it meant that Blake was now on his way out of the army, and it gave McQuillen clear sailing to his officer's commission. He had removed his prime obstacle with one masterful stroke.

Campbell said lamely, "Arnold sent me to find you.

8

Something is stirring to the east! Looks like horses on the move."

Blake leaped into the saddle and without a backward glance spurred his horse into a fast gallop. A sickness was gnawing at his heart and the drums of ECK were throbbing in his head.

Corporal Arnold wheeled his mount out of the column and slowed beside Blake. He was a stocky man in dusty blues. His wide brimmed hat hid his dark eyes and whiskered jaws.

They rode together silently for a moment, neither looking at one another. Blake knew the corporal was curious about what had happened in the brush; that every scout was awaiting the opportunity to pump Campbell.

His brain churned with turmoil but he kept his eyes solidly glued on the distant columns of dust. He tried to dismiss the image of his mistakes that pounded in his brain.

A reaction to the situation made Blake automatically turn and signal for McQuillen, riding toward the column. The sergeant rode in and waited in sullen silence. Blake said evenly, "What do you think of it, Sergeant?"

McQuillen growled, "Could be wild horses. I'll take a couple of men and ride quick patrol."

Blake pulled a telescope from his saddlebag. He saw only the blue haze rising in lonely patches over the distant hills and the bright pools of sun on the bayonet cactus. Except for the faint, whitish clouds rising out of the wild, scorched landscape there was nothing.

Snapping shut the telescope Blake twisted in his saddle. His clear yellowish eyes fixed a solid stare on McQuillen. The sergeant was one of the best scouts in the army. He had served under old Taylor in the Northwest, against Tecumseh and Black Hawk and in the Seminole War, but he

9

was a troublemaker. He had been a source of provocation to Blake throughout his service career.

"Carry out a flanker movement, sergeant!" he ordered.

McQuillen wheeled his mount away, throwing up his right arm for a signal which sent the scouts into a smooth formation, putting flankers into the brush for a half-mile or so. He was contemptuous of Blake knowing that the West Pointer had overstepped himself. The sergeant had the old army attitude that West Pointers did not understand the ruggedness of the frontier warfare, and this campaign was definitely tougher than any they had been through before. Hadn't Blake proved his ineptness to fight a wild, rugged brush operation in the Seminole War?

Blake briefly watched the sergeant then turned his attention to the columns of dust. Whoever it was had a purpose for pushing his horse in this heat. Neither Mexicans nor Indians ever rode like that in the noonday sun. This could be a trap, and McQuillen was right about that patrol. He had better send out one at once.

He looked at Jack Burkhart, the bugler, a slim, wild reckless boy of seventeen, who reminded him of Henry. He felt a growing responsibility for Jack since the tragedy, but he couldn't pinpoint the reason. "Tell the sergeant to send Zaskq and Williams forward to investigate the points of dust!" he said.

The creak of saddle leather, the thud of hooves and the acrid odor of horses were alive in his senses. Tension began to flow in his veins. The specks of dust appeared distinctively against the horizon as though a single rider was moving swiftly toward the army. Another followed and still others until he was confused. It looked as though a column of horsemen were approaching.

Lightly touching spurs to the roan's flanks, Blake rode forward signalling the scouts to fan out farther. A rider came into focus over the knoll ahead of them and paused. Suddenly Zaskq and Williams shot out of the brush and closed in on the rider.

Blake pulled up shortly between a pair of tall bayonet cactus throwing one leg across the pommel. He signalled the scouts to halt and swore sharp oaths. His heart began to pound in anticipation of the meeting between the rider and himself.

Presently a slender, blonde girl emerged from the chaparral riding easily. She wore buckskin pants and a jacket with a Colt revolver strapped to her belt and a musket in a saddle holster. Two wicked looking knives were thrust behind her belt. Her windblown sombrero hung by a rawhide string around a delicate neck revealing golden hair parted tightly in the middle and braided into long ropes that touched slim thighs.

She gouged her big bay charger into a dance alongside Blake touching stirrups. "Hello Jed," her voice was a husky rhythm filled with weariness. "I just couldn't stick it out in Corpus Christi with that bunch of crazy females!"

A tightness clamped around Blake's throat and the silence was a thick wall between them. His sympathy and understanding flowed out to this exhausted, saddle-worn girl as her sea-green eyes roved over the scouts.

He said with surprise, "It's almost thirty miles to Corpus Christi!"

She nodded. "Some Mexicans tried to stop me." Her smile was faint in a heart-shaped face that had strong features, high cheekbones and a full sensuous mouth which accentuated her clear polished flesh not yet darkened by exposure to the southwest sun. "I shot one and outran the others. Where's Henry?"

He took a deep breath, let his tongue roll around inside his mouth. Fortune Calloway was an unbridled, fierce, spoiled female but a child at heart. Being the colonel's daughter she had full run of the regiment.

Blake said. "The colonel's back with the regiment. You'd better ride back and report. If he's going to send you back to Corpus Christi somebody else will have to take you."

11

Weariness seemed to flow out of her slim body and her green eyes took on a smothered fire. "I am staying with the regiment," she announced in an irked voice.

"A field campaign isn't the place for you, Fortune. We're expecting trouble anytime."

She laughed. "What are you afraid of? That Henry will marry me instead of that lily faced Louisa Woolfolk. You and Paw are a couple of stuffy fools!"

A voice hailing them broke into their thoughts. First Lieutenant George Warren rode up with a grin on his dark, round face. "Well," he cried. "If it isn't the colonel's daughter! Ride all this way just to be with me?"

Fortune smiled as if to let him in on some intimate secret. "It's no trick for me, George. For any other woman it'd be quite a feat!"

"Some woman, eh, Blake?" Warren said admiringly.

Blake nodded as a slight irritation arose in him. He didn't like this sort of play in front of his men. "Will you take her back to the regimental headquarters?" he asked Warren.

Warren nodded and grinned. "Come along Fortune!"

She dug spurs lightly into her charger's flanks and rode off giving Blake a puzzled glance. He knew what was in her mind. How could he tell her about Henry?

He turned his gaze toward the mysterious mountains as strong feelings of desperation arose in him. He shrugged them off, and rode on watching the mountains clothed in velvet mists and the clouds casting long shadows over the desolated landscape. The eagle was a tiny speck in the sky.

He had wanted Henry to marry Louisa Woolfolk, have children and not undergo the hardships like the men of his family for the past hundred years. But Henry would have none of this—was it the strange gods of ECKANKAR who called the wild, young rebel to Texas and his death?

12

Night dropped swiftly across the semitropical land like a dark veil covering the little American army as mysteriously as the country through which it had marched that day. A rising wind moaned lonely around the white tents on the little knoll. A bright, round moon reflected in a nearby pool of deep water.

Colonel Elijah Calloway, USA, commanding the Eleventh Regiment, was eating with his daughter in the regimental tent. A lantern, swung from a rope that stretched between the two poles, made shadows dance across the white canvas tent walls.

Admiration for her glowed in his dark, brown eyes, but his lean jaws were set in a hard, determined line. He had just told her that she had to return to Corpus Christi with the first dispatch riders.

She replied firmly, "I'm not going back, Paw. I can't stand living with those simpering females!"

He looked at her steadily, loving her deeply because she was the very image of Mary, his lovely, deceased wife. For that reason alone, he was always hard put to deny her demands.

Why was she here? He dared not ask himself that question. It was evident she had followed the army across that trackless waste to be with Henry Blake. She was supposed to have returned to her aunt in upper state New York, and await the end of the war. But she wanted none of the genteel life, instead preferring the wild life of the frontier with the troops with whom she was a favorite.

He groaned inwardly, remembering Fortune had been dragged from army post to army post, watching the dull routine, the officers' acceptance of routine and red tape, and watching them become automatons during peacetime for so long that she had developed contempt for the army. When Henry Blake appeared she became attentive. He was the sort of man to win her attention, reckless and dashing, hard and bullying in his way, almost contemptuous of her.

13

The colonel said slowly, "But you can't stay. The army's pushing beyond the Nueces into Mexico, to Matamoros, and we'll have a big fight somewhere. The Mexicans don't like this invasion. They will do anything to throw us out. If we're defeated it'll be every man for himself. You know what happens to defeated armies!"

"I don't scare easily," she said.

She was like her mother. Wherever the Eleventh went, Mary went with him. Mary had been the grande dame of the regiment. If she had been alive she would have never let him err in assigning Henry to handle that patrol. It was wrong, for Henry was too reckless, too careless, and that particular patrol invited disaster for any man but a self-controlled and disciplined one. He wondered what made him do it. He could have used McQuillen or Arnold.

Calloway said, "I can't depend on General Taylor. He's too jumpy. He's liable to say that you can stay today and tomorrow order you home."

"Why, Paw?"

"Because this isn't a war. It's a political campaign. Everybody's calling it Polk's war, and the whole army's infected with politics."

She said, "I thought the General didn't have anything to do with politics?"

"As a rule he doesn't. But he's changed altogether," Calloway shook his head. "I don't understand it, myself. The other day he was denouncing the annexation of Texas, and said the Texans' claim was false, that the disputed territory belongs to Mexico and the original boundary was from the Nueces and hills ranging north from its source. He reversed himself today and has become Polk's tool in this outright invasion of Mexican territory."

She gave him a steady look knowing he was aware that she was going to stay. She could twist any officer in the army around her finger except Taylor. "I'm not worried about old Taylor," she said.

14

At the colonel's silence she thought about Henry. She had tried to model herself in his image, learning to throw the knife, handle a gun and work at all the deadly arts of killing in a grim manner. Henry only respected her when she fought him. She was now more man than woman.

Suddenly her eyes became a glittering green flame. Half-smiling she whipped out a knife. The blade glinted in the lantern light and thudded into the tent post. The colonel puffed easily on his pipe without a glance at the quivering knife.

He smiled broadly, "I'm always worried about you on these field campaigns. If I agree will you promise to respect my orders?"

"I will do whatever you wish, Paw," she replied quickly.

"That's better, but don't get any ideas about parties or dances. We're too busy for that kind of tomfoolery."

She said tiredly, "I'm not interested in that stuff. I came to be married!"

Suddenly he was filled with the beating of the drums. He half-rose with his hands out. Going to be married? The words were in rhythm with the drums beating inside him.

"What's wrong?" she cried.

The wind swept through the tent. The lanterns swung hard against the post, lighting his face in grotesque patterns. "Henry is dead!" he said hoarsely. "He was killed in an ambush three weeks ago!"

His words hung in the air. She sat remembering vividly everything around her, the empty plates, the white tent walls and the moaning of the wind. Henry dead? Impossible!

He put rough hands on her shoulders. "I had no idea you were to be married! This adds concern to the duty I've got to do!"

She whispered, "What do you mean, Paw?"

"Jed Blake's been charged with striking his sergeant over Henry's death. It's crazy, but I've got to conduct the investigation. It's been ordered by headquarters!"

15

Every fiber in her youthful body quivered. She wondered if this was a wild dream, and soon she would awake to find Henry at her side. As she slid into a dead faint the colonel gently lowered her to a nearby pallet of blankets.

Sergeant McQuillen walked through the rows of sleeping scouts in the gray dawn. "Up, bugler!" he said shaking young Burkhart. "Rustle them Mohawks out. We gotta go!"

As the early morning fog filtered in, coldly penetrating the bones of the big sergeant, he pulled his jacket around him knowing that in a couple of hours he would be discarding it. He was tired and irritable from standing the graveyard watch and his high cheek was swollen and throbbed with pain.

Grumbling, the scouts pulled out of their blankets and rolled them. Most of them tugged on their boots before washing in a nearby pond, where they snorted and splashed like animals. Hultkrans, a horse faced man with chin whiskers got some sidemeat out of his saddlebag, sliced a couple of pieces and built a fire.

McQuillen roared, "You ain't got time for that. Get over to Company A and get some java and beans, then saddle up! Pronto, man, and take the others with you!"

Hultkrans stomped out the fire. "You ain't fit to live with, Sarge," he growled. "If I'd been the looey you'd be six feet under by now!"

"You pig-headed mule!" McQuillen swore.

"The looey's comin'. Knock it off!" the bugler barked.

McQuillen turned to face Blake. He wondered how it would be to exchange his sleeve chevron for a single gold bar like that which Blake was wearing. Except for their sleeve insignia it would have been hard to distinguish either, for both wore single-breasted frock coats, fatigue caps and trousers which were a lighter colored blue.

"What's the night report, Sergeant?" Blake asked returning the salute.

McQuillen said flatly, "Williams and Zaskq are still out. They're overdue!"

"How far is it to the ford at the Arroyo Colorado?"

McQuillen returned the officer's gaze thinking how he prided himself on being a good soldier whether serving under Blake or anybody else, but Taylor was his ideal. The general was not a West Pointer and he appealed to the enlisted man's imagination. Taylor came up from the ranks by service in the Indian campaigns and was a hero to all troopers. The men worshiped old Taylor.

"About a dozen miles, sir," he replied wondering if Blake was disturbed over the incident. The officer's composure was making him irritable. "The main army ought to reach it by noon. Here come the scouts now."

Two scouts rode up and wearily dismounted. Williams, a tall Texan, approached, slapping dust out of his leather chaps. Zaskq, a slim, slighter and smaller man, went to the fireplace for coffee.

"There's a whole army of Mexicans behind the hills, Lieutenant," he said. "I think they will make a stand at the ford!"

"Report to headquarters and get back fast after eating," Blake ordered. Turning to the sergeant, he said, "Saddle up and get the men ready to ride. You take a detail out ahead!"

McQuillen rode out across the plains with a detail of three scouts, wondering if his charges would stick. It didn't seem as if he had a chance because of Blake's family background of military tradition among the older officers, Worth, Twiggs, Calloway and Scott, who had all soldiered with Blake's father in the War of 1812.

He ordered Hultkrans forward to scout the area and rode on with the other two scouts, still in thought. A half mile away from the main body of scouts he was suddenly jolted out of his reveries by a pistol shot. Hultkrans appeared out of the brush whipping his horse.

17

McQuillen halted the detail and shaded his eyes. There were puffs of musket smoke arising from the brush. Almost simultaneously a dozen red coated riders burst into view yelping shrilly like hunters after the fox. It was a panorama on a giant stage with color, action and swift horses.

McQuillen twisted his horse sharply. "Let's go," he yelled.

He lashed his mount into action, racing toward the main body of scouts with the others following. A mile back they ran into the scouts in the mesquite, where McQuillen reported; then settled back expecting a reprimand for almost getting trapped.

Blake ignored the blunder. "What direction are the Mexes?"

McQuillen pointed. At that moment Williams rode up saying the Mexican lancers had retreated eastward where there was a large body of troops encamped.

Blake signaled for the scouts to ride. They climbed the first hill without difficulty coming out on a flat high plateau where they overlooked the countryside. In the distance was the silvery thread of the Arroyo Colorado flowing through the hot land, and beyond the flat prairie was covered with the red and blue jackets of the Mexican troops.

The first brigade brought up its baggage train and parked in the rear of the army. A guard was thrown around it to await the outcome of the first major engagement between the opposing armies.

The scouts of the Eleventh kept riding in every few minutes with reports giving the same intelligence. The enemy was going to make a stand just beyond the ford. Blake sent the reports to Colonel Calloway, after a time, and shortly orders poured through the army. The Eleventh deployed to the right in battle formation.

Blake remembered that some of his scouts were still in the forward area and ordered McQuillen to reconnoiter the terrain to find them. The brisk movements around the army contrasted sharply with the hot, sleepy landscape. The musicians struck up a fast melody of Yankee Doodle, and the troops quickly fell into step with the tune.

His mind roamed for a moment. The blaring bugles, creak of saddle and movements of the army preparing for battle made his nerves tingle. He always found this particular moment, just before entering battle, most satisfactory. It made his spirits soar.

His mood was broken by the arrival of orders for the scouts to deploy. The bugler's call rang sharp and clear on the late morning air, and the movement of the scouts began, gracefully swinging out in a half circle, before the army, stretching for a half mile across the prairie.

For the last mile before reaching the ford the rising dust from the horse's hooves, and the tramping of feet mingled with the yelling of orders to the ranks, became a confusion of sounds. Blake had received a report that the Mexicans were massing a great army beyond the ford, when Peddar Zaskq, his guide for this part of the campaign in Mexico, rode up.

The scout was clad in immaculate sky blue, tight-fitting breeches, short brimmed hat and shining blue boots. He rode a black stallion with white stocking legs and his saddle and bridle were of a bluish leather embellished with silver trappings.

He spoke in a clear, ringing voice. "With your permission, Lieutenant, I'll cross the river and bring back a correct report on the enemy!"

Blake studied the smooth, brown face. The man's piercing blue eyes were like fathomless and mysterious sapphires. He wondered about this man who had so mysteriously appeared when they entered Mexico on the first leg of the campaign. He was in some way associated with the strange religion called ECKANKAR. Somehow, Blake had

19

heard that he was an American over one hundred years old. But this was a superstitious land.

Blake asked, "What about the ford?"

"Captain Lee, of the Engineers, says it's four feet deep and about eighty yards wide."

"Take Arnold with you and cross the river. Bring back anything you consider important," Blake said, wondering at this strange man who wore a pistol thrust into his belt and a holstered knife slung from his left shoulder.

After Zaskq was gone Warren reined up beside him and spoke. "Hear you got troubles for beating up your sergeant. Headquarters says you might get court-martialed!"

Blake shook his head. "First, I've heard about it!"

"It's a game, Blake. I think they pass out rumors to get you stirred up before throwing the book at you."

"What's the latest word on the battle order?" Blake asked angrily.

"General Mejia, Mexican army commander, came over to see Taylor. Said if we cross the Arroyo Colorado it means war. But Taylor said he regretted it, but he had orders to proceed to Matamoros."

Blake nodded grimly.

"Something else, friend," Warren leaned over speaking in a low whisper. "Fortune's learned about Henry's death!"

Blake's spine stiffened. His face became ash-white and his lips tightened in a long, thin line. No doubt the colonel had to tell her. Before he could speak Peddar Zaskq appeared out of the milling dust, his clothes dripping wet from the river water.

He pulled his stallion to a sliding halt. "I've been across the river," he said. "The Mexicans are retreating. There's less than three hundred left behind!"

Warren reacted sharply. "I don't believe that, Blake!" he cried. "There must be a large body of troops hiding somewhere. It's a trap. He missed them!"

"They're retreating," Zaskq said stiffly.

Blake said sharply, "Take the report to Colonel Calloway."

Warren stared at the Lieutenant while Blake scribbled the report on paper and handed it to him. The scout Peddar Zaskq was out of earshot when he spoke again. "I don't trust that fella. You shouldn't either!"

"Don't try to run my command," Blake snapped.

He turned back to the field again as Warren rode off angrily. Bugles shrilled for the army to march across the ford. Old Glory, nestling among the regimental flags, moved majestically through the ranks as the color guard stepped into the water.

Four companies of the Second Regiment, under Captain C.F. Smith, plunged into the water in perfect accord. As they struck the edge, Brigadier-General William J. Worth, commanding the Second Division, a striking and picturesque officer with a soldierly air, galloped his horse to the head of the column and led the charge across the muddy water.

The troops waded silently through the waters expecting a volley of fire but nothing happened. A squadron of dragoons, under Major Frank Dennis, followed, their red and blue uniforms and great shakos shining in the torrid sun. The entire army marched over quickly, reaching the Mexican shore within thirty minutes from the time orders were given for the movement.

When the column reached the far shore, the men cheered loudly and formed into battle order with the band striking up "Columbia, Gem of the Ocean," and the troops marched quickly up the embankment. They found only a few retreating Mexicans, and a deep underlying moan of disappointment went through the army.

Turning in his saddle Blake saw the scout Peddar Zaskq was watching him with a strange electric, blue eyed stare. The guide was right, but how did he know? The thumping like far off drums began beating in his head. He shook it trying to get rid of the queer sound.

21

Could this be the strange drums of the other worlds that Peddar called the Music of ECK — the Song of the SUGMAD?

Chapter Two

Sunlight filtered into the room warming the pink walls. A canary in a cage whistled gaily awakening the sleeping woman. She opened her dark eyes slowly and straightened her slender body under the rumpled covers with an impression that a rich white light was surrounding her.

Sitting up in bed she reached for the cup of chocolate the maid had left on the side table. While drinking it she thought of this as the eternal SUGMAD, this being a new life, a living experience she must never forget, like coming out of the darkness into light—death and resurrection as she had learned so long ago at the knee of her master Rebazar Tarzs, the great ECK Adept.

Then she remembered this was the day the American army would reach Matamoros. That Peddar Zaskq, her brother in spirit, would visit with her.

Joy bubbled through her as she rose and pulled an ochre colored gown around her and walked slowly with catlike grace to the sparkling river. A bare shoulder gleamed like polished gold in the sunlight and her long, black raven hair was pulled back and held tightly by a golden headband.

Sarita Gonzales was slender, beautiful, a symmetry of dark loveliness which set men's brains afire. Her dark haunting glance searched out the cultivated fields between the high hedges and thatched roofs of the cottages beyond

23

the river. The town consisted of low, flat sun-baked buildings pushed together, with bars on the windows. The wide streets were filled with a noisy, gay colorful crowd which cared little that the Yankee army was marching on the city.

She was happy in anticipation of seeing her friend again. She was the only living member of a family which had perished at the hands of Santa Anna's troops during the Mexican War of Independence against Spain in 1821. Santa Anna believed her family had conspired with Ferdinand VII of Spain to reconquer Mexico and had ordered the execution of the entire family. All died except herself who had escaped by the help of Rebazar Tarzs, the Tibetan ECK Adept, who had turned her over to Juquila, abbot of the ECK Order at Chizza.

A tiny brown woman glided into the room. "The Yankees are coming," she announced.

Sarita glanced at the purple horizon and saw the thin patches of dust rising against the haze. Her lids narrowed over dark, brooding eyes leaving a tiny slit partly covered by long, thin lashes, and her lips were curved pleasantly against highly polished flesh. She had the high cheekbones and the full nostrils of the mountain Indians.

She replied in a low, contralto voice, "Sí."

"General Ampudia will wipe out the Yankee dogs," the maid said gleefully.

"It is the will of the SUGMAD that the Americanos come," Sarita replied.

She remained in the door smiling as the canary sang. The carnival in the streets below became a rising clamor. Soon the first Yankees astride fine horses arrived on the far side of the river. The dull-blue clad army marched out of the blinding sun along the steep riverbank, its colors flying and bands playing lively tunes.

In sharp contrast the green and red flag of Mexico, its symbol of an eagle clutching a snake in its talons, waved gracefully from various points over the city. Sentinels

24

strolled carelessly along the levee. A few natives seated idly on the grassy banks watched the Americans settle down into camp. The Mexicans were too busy, on the whole, with their carnival to be disturbed by the arrival of the enemy.

She thought about her spiritual guide crossing the Rio Grande in its present flood stage but dismissed the flutter of anxiety and remembered they were both considered traitors and subject to arrest and death.

She bathed, powdered and dressed and took a seat on a pink divan to await his arrival knowing instinctively he would not stay long after receiving her message. They had to talk over plans of removing General Parades and his government from office, and of the personal dangers confronting them.

She wondered if the stars would fulfill the prophecy of her marriage with a white warrior from the north. Would it be some Yankee in that little army across the river? Memories of the dishonor a foreigner had wrought upon her caused the girl to shudder. But this was the will of the SUGMAD and must be followed.

Peddar Zaskq came at sundown, slim, wiry and gay. She realized that his friedship even in dire danger would never cease to be a wonder.

"The gods are good to you, Sarita," he smiled warmly.

"I thank Rebazar Tarzs for taking care of you," she said motioning toward the divan. "Your clothes are wet. Did you swim the river?"

"I did. There was no other way!"

She anxiously watched his face. "I understand the Americanos have conferred with Mejia and refused a treaty?"

"Mejia means to fight," he replied glancing sharply around the room. "Parades has sent him the Tampico Guards regiment for reinforcement. The military caste is determined to wreck Mexico by war, while France and England await the outcome to pick up new territory. Mexico may lose a good part of the country, including California to the foreigners."

"This is bad but not half as much as what I've to tell you." She studied his square face silently knowing he was already aware of why she was in Matamoros.

He nodded for her to continue.

"Santa Anna has sent his agent to Washington City to negotiate his return from exile in Cuba, to drive out Parades, make himself President, and give the Americanos a treaty to suit themselves."

"Only a fool would believe Santa Anna," he said.

She smiled sadly. "Besides, there's treachery in the army of northern Mexico. In case of defeat Mejia and Canalas will declare themselves dictators of the northern provinces and concede the Rio Grande as the boundary between Mexico and the United States."

Peddar Zaskq got up abruptly and walked to the door. Satisfied that the only person about was the little servant, he leaned over the girl again. "Talk in a low voice for even the walls have ears," he whispered. "Why are you here?"

"Juquila sent me to see the Alcalde of Matamoros. The mission could be handled only as a personal one. Rebazar Tarzs told him to send me."

"Go on."

She whispered, "I am to try to persuade him not to fortify the city for battle. It would mean useless bloodshed of women and children, the city would suffer the loss of millions of pesos, and an awful destruction in lives. A fight now might cause a catastrophe which would not stop until all Mexico is destroyed."

"Suppose the Alcalde betrays you?" he said.

"I think not," she replied. "SUGMAD'S protection is too great!"

"What else is there to do if your mission fails?"

"I am to meet with the chelas of the Master tonight and

26

try to persuade them to oppose the military leaders and sue for peace."

Peddar Zaskq nodded briefly.

"If there is war," she continued, "I have been ordered to follow the army contacting the followers of the SUGMAD, and try to influence them to make the war leaders stop fighting and bring peace to our country."

Zaskq said, "You are in danger, of course, but the hand of the SUGMAD is protecting you. But be careful, you know what would happen if Coloner Zapatos finds you here!"

"Is Zapatos in Matamoros?" she asked quickly.

"Yes, I hear," he replied rising. "I must go now!"

Her frown changed to a bright smile. "Is there nothing to tell? You always tease me about the handsome men whom you meet, hoping to make a match. Are there any in the Yankee army?"

He laughed, "I had almost forgotten. There is a Lieutenant in the Scouts. I serve under him. You will meet!"

Her heart stirred strangely. "Perhaps so, but under better circumstances."

Standing up she put a hand on his arm. "Go before anyone sees you," she said sadly. "Don't worry about me for I will take care of the mission. Don't try to return unless I send for you. Be careful how you cross the river. There is more danger from flood waters than bullets."

Peddar Zaskq returned safely to the encampment of the scouts. He laid down in the warm sands, wrapped in a blanket, to watch the stars twinkling like jewels in the dark heavens. A chilling wind from the hills made him huddle deeper into his blankets and wish that he had taken off his damp clothes. He was tired, weary and his wiry body taut from the tension of knowing that Sarita was in a precarious position.

The campfires of the American army gleamed like so many tiny pinpoints of beaded lights and the dark images of trees stood out in a fixed position around the camp.

His thoughts were irregular and obscure, on the war and his life over all these many years. Although he looked to be about thirty-five, he was far older than that.

He knew that Juquila, at the bidding of Rebazar Tarzs, had told him to act as a scout in the Yankee army, but the reason was never revealed. He was somewhat devoted to the slim, dark-eyed beauty of the mountain Indians who could command a force of thousands of warriors if Juquila would sanction it. But this depended upon the ECK, otherwise known as the SUGMAD, the God of all things.

Hard fingers dug into his shoulders and shook him. Anger stirred in Zaskq. He came up fast to find a trooper there. The soldier explained that Major Dennis, of the Third Dragoons, wanted Zaskq at the headquarters tent.

Zaskq pulled on his wet boots and followed the soldier across the shadowy field. Inside the tent a light revealed the tall, broad figure of Major Frank Dennis. A short, stocky man in a homespun coat, with a broad brimmed hat on his knee, sat in the shadows.

The major's arrogant, brown-eyed stare bore into Zaskq. "You've been with the scouts since Corpus Christi, and should know a great deal about our army by now. How does it compare with the Army of Mexico?"

"I don't know," Zaskq replied politely. "Not being a military man, I can't make comparisons."

The major picked up a long stemmed pipe and lighted it with a sulphur match. He smiled coldly but his eyes were hot. "Is it true that you are an American?"

"Yes, I am. But I have been living in Mexico for several years. I helped in the Mexican revolution against Spain. The family that I lived with was completely wiped out except for one young daughter."

28

The officer looked at the man in the shadows. Finally the other man spoke in a blunt, commanding voice. "Have you finished with the investigation of Blake's scouts?"

"Yes, General," said Dennis.

"Then why did you call Zaskq, or whatever his name is? He is not a member of the army but a civil guide. His testimony may not be accepted in court."

Zaskq looked at this man. This was General Taylor, commanding officer of the American expeditionary forces. The officer was a bit paunchy with a red, weather-beaten face, keen blue eyes, wide humorous mouth, curling hair and short sideburns. He looked more like a farmer than the General of the Army.

"I thought he might add something to the evidence," Dennis muttered.

"I should have left the investigation in Calloway's hands," Taylor grumbled. "All right, get along with your questions."

Dennis asked, "Did you see Lieutenant Blake strike the Sergeant, while on reconnaissance the afternoon before we crossed the Arroyo Colorado?"

Zaskq realized what was taking place. The major did not like Blake so he had invited the General to listen in on this talk while trying to get the guide to make a damaging admission against Blake.

"I was on patrol with Williams," Zaskq replied quietly. "I saw nothing and know nothing except what I hear."

Disappointment registered in Dennis' face. "Then tell me about the ambush in which Henry Blake got killed on March 26th."

"I don't know anything about that either, Major. I wasn't there," Peddar Zaskq said soberly.

"What do you mean?" Dennis demanded.

"I was ahead in the field. In fact I rode completely through the ambush without seeing anything. I didn't know what happened. Williams and I were about a mile ahead when the ambush happened."

29

"Did you know there were Mexicans around?"

Zaskq got hold of his temper quickly. "I reported to Corporal Blake that the enemy was somewhere in the vicinity."

Dennis puffed on his pipe. "I don't understand. Why did Lieutenant Blake insist on his brother taking that patrol? That kid was too hairbrained for any command."

Taylor's voice interrupted sharply. "Why are you taking to conducting an investigation alone? Where are the other members of the board?"

Dennis flushed. "Ringgold's sick, Calloway's on duty and Wilson's been assigned to General Headquarters tonight. But Blake is guilty for almost every scout has testified against him. Campbell saw him strike McQuillen. And Blake has been in hot water for a long time. He ought to be drummed out of the service!"

"I'm not worried about Blake," Taylor replied testily taking a cheroot out of his vest pocket. "Let the court decide that. Meanwhile we'd better think about the position we're facing. Our force is altogether too small for the accomplishment of its mission. Looks as if Scott deliberately sent us out with such a small army so that we'd get massacred and bring on a war."

"I can prove that Blake is guilty, sir," Dennis proclaimed loudly.

"Prove it in court," Taylor snapped. "Where's Worth and Twiggs? I sent for them a half hour ago. Seems they would stop arguing long enough over who is going to succeed me in the command of this army to find out what we're faced with!"

He waved impatiently. "Take this man and get out. Send another runner for Worth and Twiggs. We've got work to do before the Mexes come down on us with a bigger force and wipe us out!"

Outside in the cold, windy darkness Dennis turned on the guide. "You should have cooperated with me, Zaskq!"

"I told you the truth, Major," Zaskq replied quietly.

Dennis said bitterly, "How'd we know you didn't lead Corporal Blake's detail into that ambush? You might even be a spy!"

Zaskq smiled wryly. "I deny both of your accusations."

A deep tension flowed out from the officer. "I'm aware that you went into Matamoros today." Triumph rose in his voice. "Can you prove why you took the trip? Did you have permission? Whom did you see there, and for what reason?"

Zaskq took a step backwards. He took control of himself. "I went over to see a woman, Major," he said mockingly. "Does that make me a spy?"

Dennis' brittle laughter filled the darkness. "Prove it, Zaskq," he said in an iron-hard voice. "Your boots and pants are wet. How else would they be wet except by swimming your horse across the river?"

He turned sharply and was swallowed up in the night. Zaskq stared for a few moments in the direction the officer had taken. He shrugged and walked slowly toward the bivouac of the scouts thinking that Dennis was trying to put him in a trap.

Blake and Williams returned from a reconnaissance close to midnight, and settled down for coffee at the campfire where a big pot nestled in the deep glowing fire. Williams went to his blankets while Blake lingered over a second cup of coffee. He was tired, but wanted to think.

Gradually his mind stilled and the sounds of the night poured over him. Nearby horses snorted impatiently and stomped around the makeshift corral.

Blake rose and went to the corral of fenced horses and whistled softly. The roan came up and nosed him in the darkness with its wet muzzle. He stroked the neck and rubbed the head of the beautiful animal softly as thoughts stirred deeply in himself.

31

Out of the night came the call of the sentries mingling faintly with the breathing of an army that slept soundly. The yowling of coyotes and the steady humming song of the night insects drowned out the voices from headquarters. Everything in the service was a part of himself. It was as if he had suddenly been thrust outside of himself and was able to watch all his mind and body working. The faint sounds of the drums came again. What was this? He had never before felt like this. Was it part of the great experience in ECKANKAR which Peddar Zaskq had spoken about?

The roan snorted and pulled away. Blake looked up to see Zaskq step silently into the rim of firelight and seat himself on a log.

He was pouring a cup of coffee when Blake came up. "Good evening, Lieutenant," he said pleasantly.

"You're up late, Zaskq," Blake frowned. "Something wrong?"

Zaskq smiled easily. "Nothing, Lieutenant. There's a rumor going around that some 25,000 Mexican troops are on their way from Tampico to join those across the river."

"Just talk," Blake commented sitting down. "Does Polk deliberately plan to provoke a war in the interest of slavery by putting us here on the Rio Grande?"

"Perhaps Polk thinks that by taking possession of the disputed territory he has put his country in a stronger position to negotiate, and if the Mexicans don't agree it gives us a good base for operations."

"You're right, Zaskq, but we can't fight two wars. Polk has frightened the British out of the Oregon country with his claims of fifty-four forty or fight talk. If England decides to fight we're in for a bad time."

Zaskq finished his coffee and looked at Blake with brooding eyes. "I am restless tonight. One of my best friends, a young woman, is in Matamoros."

"Is she safe?" Blake asked in surprise looking at Zaskq's damp boots.

Zaskq followed the glance. "She can take care of herself, so my worry is needless. She's under the protection of our God, the Supreme SUGMAD!"

"She is Mexican?"

"She is an Indian, a descendent of the race out of which Quetzalcoatl sprang."

The guide got up to leave, but paused. "I must tell you, Lieutenant, I was called to headquarters and questioned by Major Dennis about your quarrel with Sergeant McQuillen."

"Why did he do that?" Blake asked sharply.

Zaskq shrugged and told what had happened at the headquarters. He finished and disappeared into the night.

Blake stared at the fire wondering what this meant. Raising his eyes to the cold stars he whispered a prayer, but quick steps interrupted his mood. He turned and found Fortune Calloway with great sadness reflecting in her sea-green eyes standing beside him.

She murmured, "What did you have to do with Henry's death?"

Something pathetic about her made him take her hand. She was a child and this was a dream. But he shook his head.

"They say you forced Henry to take that patrol. Is it true?"

"No," he said quietly watching the firelight play on her face. "I did not. When I heard that Henry was assigned to the patrol, I volunteered to take it. The Colonel refused because he couldn't spare me. I don't know how these rumors get started."

Her eyes became blazing pools. "You are trying to put the blame on Paw!" she cried.

He stepped back from her sudden fury. Her hand struck his cheek with such an impact it rattled him. She glared at him with hot, white intensity. Suddenly she whirled off into the darkness.

Fortune arrived at her tent and flung off her clothes in the dark. She jumped into the cot but sleep was impossible for her thoughts kept churning around in her brain like a steamboat wheel.

A chilly gust of wind swept through the tent. She opened her eyes and looked at the heavy, windy darkness of her canvas abode. The wind crawled under the cot like a dark, malignant creature on steady feet. A shuddering coldness went through her thin, leggy body.

Lightning streaked across the sky and the tent became as brilliant as day and the wind whooped again under the cot laying dark fingers across her. The flaps came open and fluttered letting in gushes of air. She rose and started fastening them while thinking of Jed and Henry Blake. Something indefinable worked faintly in her brain tugging and pulling at her thoughts.

Pebbles rattled along the path and she shrank back thinking it might be Jed Blake. "Miss Fortune," Sergeant McQuillen's heavy voice reached out of the raw, windy night.

She gave a start as a lantern jiggled along the path throwing its faint light against the gusty darkness. Sergeant McQuillen stood before her like some prehistoric monster in the inky night. His eyes glowed like an animal's in the darkness.

Hastily she pulled her night wrap together. "The storm aroused me," she explained. "I was tying the flaps. What are you doing this close to the headquarters?"

"I have been out looking after the horses. The storm disturbed them." He stood silently looking at her. Down through the hills and prairies swept the wind crying and howling, lifting the tents and slamming canvas to the earth. "That wind sure came up fast," he added.

She could hardly speak for fear her voice would betray the pain ripping through her. "Yes," she murmured.

McQuillen said abruptly, "You know what happened to Henry?"

"Paw told me," she whispered.

"It ain't natural, Miss Fortune. Just ain't natural for that wild young'un not to be with us. Some says it was the weirdo guide we have, that put the patrol into that ambush. His name's Zaskq. But I just don't rightly know."

She asked herself, would McQuillen have nerve enough to say what was on his mind at the court-martial? She knew the sergeant to be a strange person, but a real trooper and an avenging angel in battle. Yet aside from fighting he lived and dreamed a commission until it had become a form of sickness.

"Made up your mind what to say at the court?" she asked suddenly.

He shifted his feet wondering if she could see his swollen face in the darkness. "All I know about that ambush is what's been barracks talk. Wouldn't put a five cent piece of stock in it. But the court ain't for that. It's going to be held 'cause Blake hit me."

The cold wind swooped through the tent again cutting her flesh. "I'd like to know the truth about Henry's death. From what I've heard, Blake talked Henry into taking that patrol. You say it could be that guide's fault. What's the truth, Sergeant?"

McQuillen smiled faintly. "I don't rightly know, Miss Fortune. But if them rumors keep up like they've been, there's something wrong. Where there's smoke, there's fire!"

"Good night, Sergeant," she said abruptly pulling the curtains together.

The words were thick chunks of air in her throat. She sat on the cot listening to the gale wailing across the prairie. The horses thudded restlessly about the corral. Cracks of thunder rattled spasmodically across the heavens.

Looking up suddenly fear rushed through her veins. Standing in the corner was a dark figure. A blot of darkness, against the black of the inner space of the tent. She jumped up. A face gleamed briefly.

"Henry!" she cried.

Thunder roared across the sky and the shrieking wind tore through the mesquite. Enormous raindrops pounded heavily against the earth. She flung back the curtains to find the figure had disappeared. She was a stark figure in a windswept gown, standing, frightened face raised up to the black sky.

The pounding wind drove her back into the tent. Weeping she fell across the cot, crying his name. The rain crashed down in a blinding deluge.

Chapter Three

The hot, bright rays of the morning sun spreading across the brown hills sparkled in the surging river waters. Jed Blake supervising the scouts in the digging of trenches and construction of fort walls, felt the sultry heat bite into his flesh.

The scouts bitterly resented the detail but Taylor had ordered every available man in the army to be put to work in the construction of Fort Texas which he intended to establish as a permanent base opposite Matamoros. Blake stood and watched and brooded over his service career which hinged upon the outcome of the forthcoming court-martial.

He pulled his cap low over his eyes and let his glance swing toward McQuillen to wonder at what length the sergeant would go to crush all obstacles between himself and an officer's commission. But at this point Taylor's orderly arrived to inform him there was a meeting of the general staff in the headquarters tent.

Blake turned the detail over to McQuillen and proceeded to headquarters to find most of the staff officers gathered there. Taylor, his countenance aflame with sunburn, lips peeled and dressed in blue jeans sat quietly at a table awaiting the arrival of the rest of his staff.

Lieutenant Braxton Bragg, a small dark man, in charge of the light battery, Third Brigade, was talking with Colonel Hitchcock, commander, Third Infantry. "We're paying

37

eight to ten dollars a head for mules. Sam Grant thinks the traders are cheating us, for a mule shouldn't cost over five dollars each."

"Looks like we're losing the campaign without a fight," Hitchcock, a square, florid man, snorted. "We ought to be ashamed of ourselves for mixing in this affair. But we've done it since '35 when Gaines occupied Nacogdoches. What the Mexicans have done wrong was to make Texas a mere state which gave it the right of revolution, but the boundary was established only to the Nueces. The other mistake was the cold-blooded massacre of the Texans at Goliad and the Alamo!"

"Gentlemen!" Taylor's blunt voice sounded above the murmuring din. "It's time we get down to business!"

He paused as the attention of every officer in the tent swung around to him, then continued. "We've had several events in the past few days which lead up to a major crisis. Colonel Cross, our quartermaster, was murdered while on a ride near camp. Porter's men were almost wiped out in an ambush and Walker's rangers surprised and half either killed or captured.

"Two days ago we heard that a large body of Mexicans were crossing the river some twenty-five miles upstream. I sent Captain Thornton with sixty mounted infantrymen, including some dragoons and riflemen. For some reason Major Dennis included himself in the party without orders. They ran straight into an ambush and lost a considerable number of men and the rest captured. Now Dennis, Thornton and Hardee are in a stinking jail in Matamoros."

Turning his keen gaze upon Colonel David E. Twiggs, commander Second Dragoons, he asked roughly, "Did you authorize Dennis to ride reconnaissance with Thornton, Hardee, and your men?"

"I didn't know anything about this matter until this morning," Twiggs, a big, ruddy, white haired man boomed.

Taylor puffed on his pipe. "Things have gone haywire around here. The troops are getting cut up in small parties by the Mexicans. Worth pulled out for the states, and things are in bad shape."

Blake felt the impact of antagonism which swept the little band of officers. Brigadier-General William J. Worth had quarreled with Taylor over the proper succession of command, and left angrily for Washington City to protest. He claimed the right to succeed Taylor, who was soon to retire, by seniority over Twiggs.

It was an affront to the service to speak of a high-ranking officer in the tone of voice Taylor used. Almost every officer in the tent was a West Pointer and professional soldier who fought with Worth through the War of '12 and frontier campaigns.

The atmosphere was thick with hostility as Taylor calmly turned to Colonel Calloway. "What do you know about this, Calloway?"

"When news came about the Mexican's movement downstream I requested permission from headquarters to send the Eleventh's scouts to investigate but got no reply. That's all I know," the colonel replied.

"The harm's already done," Taylor said gruffly, but slowly, punctuating his words. "For the attack is a declaration of war."

"War?" somebody murmured.

"Yes, war!" Taylor thundered thumping his fist on the table. "I've written to the president and sent copies to Marcy, the war secretary and General Scott. Captain Porter, the Gulf Fleet commander, has been instructed to establish a tight blockade of the Rio Delta. And every officer and private will hold himself ready for instant action!"

He paused letting his words sink into the minds of his officers. "Orders of the day are to prepare all field units, except the Seventh Infantry and its battery, to march to Point Isabel tomorrow morning. We'll also take the sick and their baggage and return with supplies and ammunition. Good day, gentlemen."

39

Blake returned to his detail thinking that many would never return home for what bad water and disease wouldn't kill the knives and bullets of the Mexicans would. But to his surprise none of the scouts were at work. Looking around he saw the whole camp was deserted.

Sounds of boisterous laughter from the waterfront led him through rows of white tents where curtains flapped softly in the breeze, to the riverbank. There he found the troops gathered in hard knots craning their necks at a group of young Mexican women bathing in the water on the Matamoros side.

His attention was drawn instantly to a dusky skinned girl who appeared almost simultaneously at the edge of the levee above the bathers. She was like a bronze statue, poised against the brilliant blue skyline in a strange, golden gown with tiny silhouetted figures around the edge and a bright headband pulled tightly around black hair.

An awed hush descended upon the Americans as she threw up her right hand pointing to the vast, blue bowl of heaven with a ringing cry as though a challenge to the invading army.

The bathers stopped, quickly climbed out of the dark waters to disappear over the embankment like lumbering animals. For a brief moment the girl stood facing the Americans with a long, searching glance that held them spellbound, then slipped away as quickly as she had appeared.

His brain was afire as Blake turned instinctively to find Peddar Zaskq beside him, frowning darkly. The guide interrupted his thoughts. "Yes, Lieutenant, the Mexican women always bathe in public. It is an ancient custom."

"But the girl? Who is she?" Blake asked curiously, wondering at the strange excitement in his heart.

The frown knotted on Zaskq's brown. There seemed to be something mysterious within his eyes, beyond words. "The beautiful girl? Ah yes," he murmured. "She is my spiritual sister, in ECK!"

40

Blake studied the hot landscape as he led the scouts out of the fort into open country, the same day, while thinking of the wild land that lay southward in the heart of Mexico. He rubbed his left jaw in reflection, his thoughts saying the horizon would never be reached for it always faded into the distance, receding before him as he advanced into time. Maybe this was part of the philosophy called ECKANKAR?

The army had received orders at one o'clock that afternoon for the troops to halt work on the trenches and prepare for the march to Point Isabel. As Blake gave the order his men threw away their shovels and raced for camp, whooping.

He followed at a slower pace with the bugler walking behind, wondering at the news. Taylor had heard the Mexicans were below the fort on this side of the river and had decided to march at once. Point Isabel was in an untenable position and haste had to be made to reach there before the Mexicans made an assault and destroyed all provisions and munitions for the campaign.

Tents came down hurriedly, and the wagon train made ready, and at half past three the army marched leaving the Seventh Infantry commanded by Major Brown, with Captain Lowd's four eighteen-pounders, and Lieutenant Bragg's field battery, under orders to hold out as long as possible.

Fortune Calloway, her hair like spun gold in the afternoon light, galloped past with the Second Dragoons. She saw him and turned a hot, green glance in his direction, causing Blake to speculate whether the colonel knew if she was riding with the troops.

Fortune was a merry child having an adventure and he could easily fall in love with her, but knew that his feeling must be held in abeyance for she was headstrong and would cause grief and pain. What would become of her? With these unhappy thoughts he signaled for the scouts to fan out, and gouged his roan into a quicker pace.

41

They rode through the brassy glare of the day and bivouacked with the army beside the road at sundown. Blake ate alone before a roaring fire thinking about the Mexican girl at Matamoros. Shortly he received orders to report to the regimental headquarters. He brushed off his clothes wondering at the order and walked to the headquarters tent where he found Colonel Calloway sitting outside, on a box in his undershirt, galluses hanging down.

The colonel opened in a laconic voice. "I've got troubles, son. Besides having politics to infilter my command, even our men are deserting."

"More desertions, Colonel?" Blake asked in surprise.

"Fifteen went over to the enemy last night. They swam. Think they'd have better sense after the reports coming back that the Mexes are sending them to labor in a salt mine."

"Who's behind this, Colonel?"

Calloway said, "Riley, a sergeant in the Third. Remember him?"

"He soldiered under me in the northwest!"

"He went over to the Mexes some time ago, and helps them to get our men by appealing to their religious side. Lots of Irish Catholics in the Eleventh," the colonel hawked noisily and spat on the ground.

The indiscretion displayed by the old officer made slow anger stir in Blake. "Let me have it, Colonel," he said bluntly. "Am I going to get a full sentence and be dismissed from the service?"

"I don't know," the colonel wagged his head. "I talked with Taylor yesterday to get him to call off the court, but he's stubborn about West Pointers. Looks like you might get the book unless Bill Bliss takes an interest. He's the only one who has influence with Taylor."

"Did you get my request for transferring McQuillen out of the scouts?"

"I got it, but Taylor says no. Seems like he thinks McQuillen is a good scout whether we do or not."

"By God," swore Blake angrily. "Doesn't he realize the trouble I'll have with McQuillen until the court convenes?"

Calloway shrugged his shoulders. "He said emphatically there would be no change in the scouts until this mess is cleared up!"

"Well, thanks for your troubles, Colonel!"

"Don't get sore at me, Blake. I'm only trying to help you for old times' sake. Your daddy saved my scalp at Chippewa when old Scott whipped the pants off the British."

"I'm sorry, Colonel," Blake said still half resentful.

"That's better, but since you have taken that attitude, I'll be pretty plain. The talk about you isn't good."

"So I hear," Blake smiled crookedly. "But you know I'll have to testify that I volunteered for that patrol, if I should be asked."

"I can't expect you to do otherwise," the old man said firmly. "But I doubt if the court will get sidetracked off on Henry's death."

Blake looked steadily at the colonel in the soft twilight. Neither had openly discussed that Florida fracas where Blake lost nine men in a Seminole ambush before firing a shot. The colonel had issued the order from headquarters to take that blind patrol into the swamp, and Calloway was aware of it. A parallel event was reconstructed in the disaster which took his brother's life.

Blake said bitterly, "Why couldn't McQuillen have taken the patrol instead of Henry? Were you aware that McQuillen was drunk that afternoon and couldn't be found?"

"I don't know anything about that," Calloway said evenly. "But the court won't need that kind of information. It's your trial for striking McQuillen."

Feet crunching in the sand brought Blake around. He found Fortune staring with wide eyes like green, glowing flames. "What's this about Henry?" she demanded.

"It's none of your business, daughter," the colonel interrupted firmly. "Now leave us be and don't come back until I send for you."

"I'd like to know the truth," she said dropping a hand on the knife handle in her belt.

"None of that, Fortune!" Calloway said sharply.

She slowly backed away, her eyes a sea of fire, curiously bent on Blake. Cold chills moved along his spine. He wondered if she actually believed he planned the murder of his brother? He felt her hatred almost engulfing him.

The colonel dismissed him at once. Blake returned to his bivouac sorely troubled. The drums started pounding in his head again.

Taylor led his army in a formed march of thirty miles over a hot, dry country the second day. Just before reveille of the third day the guns of Fort Texas were heard. The artillery boomed all morning loud enough to be heard by the troops marching toward Point Isabel. The troops speculated among themselves about the precarious position in which they had left their comrades. Blake, however, did not share in the growing anxiety for those left at the fort, instead his mind was focused on his own troubles.

During the midmorning Peddar Zaskq rode up to report for Williams who had remained in the field. After the guide was finished, Blake said, "I was surprised to hear you had ties on the Mexican side."

The man's eyes veiled, "Yes, Lieutenant," he replied. "Perhaps you will meet my friend someday."

"I thought you only had friends among the government circles in Mexico City? Who is this young woman? Does she live here?"

"Sarita Gonzales is a leader among her people. She must go wherever the call comes to help them," Zaskq spoke in a low voice. "She is here to rally the citizens against the military dictatorship of Mexico and bring peace. If she succeeds there will be no war with the United States. Her home, as you desire to know, is deep in the heart of Mexico. A place that is not known to those except the followers of ECKANKAR!"

With that the guide wheeled his horse and rode away. Blake stared after him surprised at the knowledge that somebody in Mexico was trying to prevent the bloodshed and horrors of war.

The army arrived at Point Isabel at noon the third day and the troopers went directly to their quarters to rest after the grueling march. Many were in an agitated state thinking the fort would be wiped out before they could return. Several officers openly accused Taylor of deliberately marching the army out of the fort in order to save it, and planning to sail for Corpus Christi.

Blake had his troubles, too, for McQuillen had disagreed with Peddar Zaskq over a field report concerning the movement of the Mexican army but Williams interfered by agreeing with the guide. Shortly afterward Warren arrived at the officer's quarters to inform Blake about the incident.

"You're going to have real trouble if you don't get rid of that guide," Warren said with hostility in his voice.

Blake replied tersely, "I heard about that but figured it didn't amount to much for both were letting off steam. We're under a big tension here. I overlook that sort of thing for it happens constantly among the scouts."

"I don't understand you, Blake!"

"Look here Warren. My men have their troubles especially under battle conditions. I just don't put my nose into anything that doesn't concern me."

Warren said bitterly, "Why do you protect Zaskq? It might get you into trouble. Maybe McQuillen is tough and out to get you for blocking him from a commission, but he's good and an American. We are not sure about Zaskq. He could be anything. Maybe a Mexican spy!"

"Your imagination is working overtime, Warren," Blake smiled. "Come, let's have a drink!"

The next morning the army received orders to stand by for its return march to Fort Texas but the order failed to materialize for the baggage train did not finish loading the munitions before sundown.

That evening Captain Walker, a ranger with Hayne's Company of Texans, arrived at Point Isabel, with some of his scouts, bringing dispatches from Major Brown. Within a few minutes a crowd of troopers was gathered before headquarters to learn what had happened at the fort.

Shortly Taylor stepped from the door and stood in the flaming light of torches. "You want to know what's going on at Fort Texas," he said. "Major Brown informs me that the fort has been under constant enemy artillery fire for three days.

"The Mexicans have fired nearly fifteen hundred rounds of balls and shells into the fort without producing the least effect. Our troops using their eighteen-pounders have silenced most of their batteries. Sergeant Mumford, of the Seventh Regiment, is the only battle casualty. He was killed by a bursting shell! Ready yourself to march at dawn to relieve Fort Texas!"

Silence followed the announcement. Then a ringing cheer burst from the troops as Taylor stepped back into his quarters with a flush reddening his cheeks. The strange sound of the drums began to beat in Blake's head. He listened carefully to the sound wondering what it meant.

46

The white clouds sailing across the deep, azure sky made patterns of light and shade over the long slopes of the hot, brown hills as Blake led his scouts along the road to Fort Texas.

There was a sharp briskness in the air on this hot afternoon of May 5, 1846 as the troops left Point Isabel on its march to Fort Texas. There was an absolute change from the previous day when many accused Taylor of deserting the fort in order to save the army from disaster.

As soon as the little army was out of the vicinity of the military establishment, Blake ordered McQuillen to take three scouts and reconnoiter the position of the enemy reported to be in the area and gathering for a battle. He watched the sergeant ride off with Arnold, Campbell and Ichler while rubbing his right cheek, glad to be rid of him for awhile.

Turning idly in the saddle Blake's clear yellow eyes roved over the marching army. This was a hard fighting army which paid more attention to its weapons than the appearance of its uniforms. Ahead of the troops rode some of the Texas scouts in their red shirts, trousers belted at the waist and buckskin caps or sombreros, each with a heavy rifle, powder horn, Bowie knife and Colt revolver. Following them came the dragoons in their scarlet coats, dark trousers, flat-topped caps or high shakos. They were the elite troops of the army equipped with broad sabers, muskets in slings and horse pistols. With them rode the mounted rifles in dark uniforms with their percussion rifles and Colt army revolvers.

The infantry marched in a crazy route step. Most of the uniforms were the conventional dark blue frocks and lighter blue trousers, except for the volunteers whose clothes made Blake shudder with disgust. They wore just about anything least resembling a uniform. Ragged, torn and constantly yelling they disintegrated all the discipline an army had. They cursed their officers and frequently got out of hand.

47

Most regiments wore the ugly, flat-topped fatigue cap, but some, including the volunteers, preferred the traditional high shako of the War of 1812. Several officers were wearing a ridiculous high cylindrical hat that resembled a stovepipe with a cap bill, including an ornamental cockade.

Brigadier General Zachary Taylor, field commander of the American army in Mexico, rode at the head of his little army on his war horse, Old Whitey. He was dressed in the odd attire of an old straw hat, blue jeans and a black frock coat that made him look more like a farmer than a soldier. Colonel William W. S. Bliss, his son-in-law, army headquarters adjutant, nicknamed "Perfect" Bliss, rode beside him. Behind was Taylor's staff.

The day was extremely hot and many of the troopers fell out every few steps despite Taylor's orders for the entire infantry regiments to stay in close formation. The men kept up a crazy sort of marching which almost drove their officers to despair.

Peddar Zaskq rode up to report. "The enemy's at a place several miles ahead called Palo Alto. I think they have about eight thousand troops under General Aristo, who has taken over command from Ampudia. They believe the American cavalry can't shoot, nor control their horses, and the infantry are needy foreigners whose appetites outdo their training."

Blake smiled. "Aristo has lots to learn about American troops, but we are in serious trouble. Every infantry colonel except Calloway and a couple of others is absent. One regiment hasn't a single field officer, another only a captain. In general, the officers lack harmony and spirit, and the troops are discontented, hopeless, unwilling to fight and weak from too much drinking at Corpus Christi!"

He paused and added. "Look at them now. Crazy as a herd of cattle on the trail where there's no water!"

"There's an explanation, Lieutenant," Zaskq said looking at the troops. He had seen men act like that before on

48

marches under a blazing sun. He had a wisdom—a divine wisdom—that was almost too canny to let come forth to others. "They are sensing a fight."

"Yes," Blake said wondering at the curiosity which aroused questions in him about this strange guide. "Tell me, Zaskq. Why were your clothes damp that evening you came to me about Dennis questioning you? Had you been across the Rio that night?"

Peddar Zaskq's piercing blue eyes flashed a meaningful glance at Blake who realized that whatever the reason was nothing would be revealed until the proper time.

The drums began to pound in his head.

Chapter Four

"The wagon train is ready to roll again, sir," Lieutenant Lester Douglas, aide to colonel Calloway, said saluting.

Calloway pulled on his leather gloves studying the young officer while he wondered why the army insisted on sending green kids to the frontier. They were never of any use to the army except for shuffling papers for a year or two in the War Department. He sighed silently while running his hands alternately around the wrists.

He growled. "I'm going to chop somebody's head off the next time a wagon hub breaks." He turned toward the long train of wagons. "Let's take a look at it!"

The torrid sunlight beat down on his back as he hunched his thin shoulders and walked swiftly toward the wagons, the aide tagging hurriedly behind him. Annoyed, the colonel wanted to turn and yell at him but remembered that military etiquette prevented it.

He was old and tired, and his long years on the frontier, the long, hard marches, fever in the swamps, a wily foe that struck and disappeared before a gun could be raised had left him a weary man. Now there was the campaign in the desert, Mary gone, and Fortune here to raise further problems. He wondered why Mary had to leave him.

He spoke over his shoulder. "Where's Fortune?"

"In the wagon train with Mrs. Kelly, sir," Douglas replied. "I put her there personally, like you told me, sir!"

51

The kid was going to sir him to death. "Good! See that she stays there. Don't want to make a camp follower out of her!" He smiled to himself as if it could be done — not that girl — she was too much like Mary. Someday she would be the grande dame of the Regiment, the Eleventh, for certain!

Reaching the line of wagons for the Eleventh, the old officer inspected the repaired axle of the munitions van. Satisfied with the repairs he returned to his horse and remounted.

Sitting there briefly Colonel Elijah Calloway looked at the line of horsemen and infantry troops awaiting his command to march. This moment was complete satisfaction for the treatment received from General Winfield Scott and other high ranking officers. A Lieutenant Colonel with almost thirty years of military service was improper. It was time he got a full colonelcy and be given a brigade. Most of those with whom he had served throughout his military career were either brevet brigadier generals or full colonels and had responsible commands.

He became aware that his aide was staring at him and looked around with a conspicuous feeling. He ordered the bugler to blow the march and simultaneously the whole regiment moved forward.

The troops were a blue twisted line with dust rising from the pounding of feet. An oppression caused by the monotony of the glaring sun over the brown landscape filled his mind. With each hoofbeat of his horse his inner self revolted at this hot world, a world which seemed as if time had halted the centuries and left it in a primordial state.

"Wish I could save him," Calloway said.

"Speaking to me, sir?" his aide asked.

"Just thinking out loud. Hoping I could do something for Blake. But there doesn't seem to be anything that anybody can do for him."

"He's in a tough spot, sir."

Calloway said, "Blake didn't have any business hitting his sergeant. Taylor's death on mistreatment of his men.

I got a lot of respect for Blake. His paw and me soldiered against the British in '12. He saved my scalp but I haven't done anything to repay him. I done Blake a wrong instead. It was down in Florida..."

He drowsed a moment to the rocking gait of his horse, then opened his eyes. "Douglas, you're a pretty smart, young fellow. Got your whole life before you. Make something out of it. Don't throw it away. Love the army like I've loved it. Be loyal in spite of anything that happens. It's a good life, but the politicians have just about ruined the army."

He broke off suddenly. "You said Fortune was with Mrs. Kelly?"

"She is!" The young officer followed the Colonel's finger. "No, by God she ain't. What's she doing with the dragoons?"

The boy spurred off but came back shortly looking defeated.

After seven miles of marching the army was halted and bedded down for the night. It moved again the following morning under the blistering sun like a gigantic sluggish serpent. Blake rode ahead with the scouts, ruminating on the report that the Mexicans were three miles ahead at Palo Alto, a group of tall trees by the road.

Taylor ordered a halt and the troops fell out around a bubbling spring. Blake motioned for the sergeant and rode away several hundred yards ahead to survey the landscape through his telescope. Far ahead a long dark line stretched across the prairie. Sun glistened on the bayonets and spearheads of the Mexican troops. He handed the long glass to McQuillen who looked and nodded his great head. His pale eyes sparkled in anticipation of battle.

The army rested, then marched again proceeding quietly

along the road for a couple of miles, halting briefly at ponds for water, then deploying in battle order. Blake's scouts were in advance of the Eleventh which had been moved into the front of the army. They continued within a mile of the enemy's lines before deploying again.

The Eleventh went to the right of the American lines, followed by the Fifth, then Ringgold's battery, the Third and Fourth infantries, two eighteen pounders under Churchill, the eleven companies of artillery, the Eighth Infantry, and on the extreme left was Duncan's battery protected by the Dragoons with whom Fortune was riding.

Action began at three o'clock with a cannonading from the Mexican's right flank, soon followed by guns at intervals through their entire lines. Ringgold's and Duncan's batteries were thrown forward replying with a deadly fire. The enemy's cannonballs played briskly through the American ranks, but the wounded and dying troops had little effect on the discipline of the army as they advanced upon the foe.

The American eighteen pounders opened at the same time with the enemy's firing to produce confusion in the Mexican's center line. Then a large body of cavalry emerged from the Mexican's left moving toward the American's right flank with the intention of turning it.

Immediately Blake sent word of the movement to Colonel Calloway. He watched the Eleventh Regiment march rapidly to the right and front to intercept the Mexican cavalry. After a swift movement of more than a fourth of a mile the Eleventh was halted and formed a square, the troops standing shoulder to shoulder while facing the onrushing enemy. Eight hundred riders in bright red uniforms, with silken pennants fluttering in the wind, waving sabers and short muskets charged their splendid horses upon the little band of Americans. A hundred feet away the horsemen discharged a sharp volley and continued their charge. A few Americans fell but the line held firmly delivering a fire with precision and a withering effect.

Blake and his scouts joined the charge with Walker's Rangers, from the flank, firing their Colt revolvers with cool, deadly aim. The Mexican charge melted away to the left and swerved in a swift hot run leaving behind a field of scattered dead and riderless horses running wildly over the battlefield.

Lieutenant Ridgely brought up two pieces from Major Ringgold's battery to the rear of the Eleventh, and as the ground would not allow them to pass, the regiment made a swift side movement to let the artillery pour its deadly grape and canister into the enemy cavalry to completely rout it.

The cannonade continued until night closed in when the spectacle was magnificent. The prairie was burning brightly between the two armies and some twenty pieces of artillery thundered from left to right, while through the bright flames came the trampling of horses and the wild shouting of troops from both sides.

After dark the American baggage train was brought up and parked on the battlefield and the men laid down on their arms to rest until dawn. The moon came up, round and bright, covering the tragic scene where they had fought that day. Taylor called for a council of his officers, in which Blake listened to the majority urge that they throw up fortifications or return to Point Isabel, for the Mexicans had twice as many troops as the Americans and defeat seemed to be in store for them.

Old Taylor gave them a keen sweeping gaze, letting it rest briefly on Blake. The scout felt a deep thrilling emotion pour through himself as the commander-in-chief said, "We'll attack at dawn." Then paused and spoke again. "I'll go ahead or stay in my boots!"

Every man knew it was old "Rough and Ready's" way of saying he would die in the attempt to reach Fort Texas.

Blake walked with Warren back to the field where the men lay scattered in sleep. They passed the parked trains of wagons from which came the sounds of anguished groans of the wounded. Overhead the stars gleamed faintly through the lurid flame colored clouds. The fires still blazed beyond the enemy's lines.

Warren said soberly, "That brilliant flank movement of the Eleventh today might have put old Zach in position for the next presidential nomination on the Whig ticket."

"I don't think either Polk or Scott would like that," Blake replied as they came into the hospital area which was lighted by huge bonfires. The wounded lay scattered over the ground like sticks in the firelight. Doctors and medical corpsmen were busy working over the stricken men.

Blake's glance lighted upon Fortune Calloway arranging a bandage on a soldier's bloody head. A strange, cold feeling arose in him as their eyes met in a fixed stare. She silently turned to her task neither smiling nor speaking.

He passed on with sudden pain churning in his stomach for that hostility in her glance told him that he faced other dangers besides those from Mexican bullets or a court-martial sentence.

The long purple banners of the day streaking the eastern sky heralded the rising sun. Sergeant McQuillen frowned heavily as he moved among the sleeping scouts to arouse them.

He stopped beside the guide, smiled grimly, and rubbing his hands against his buckskin pants, placed a foot against Peddar Zaskq's hip and shoved. The guide's china blue eyes flew open. Instantly he was on his feet with a glittering knife in his hand. The shock of the man's aggressiveness forced McQuillen to retreat quickly.

They stared at one another for a moment. Then McQuillen broke away, spinning on his heels and shouting, "All right, you Mohawks, rise and shine for we got more Mexes to lick before getting to the Fort. Hey, Campbell get outa that sack!"

He walked away rubbing his hands along his pant legs gleefully, an old habit when excited. His blood was filled with battle fever for McQuillen was in his element, the array of war where cruelty, fierce passions and murder came to the surface. His mind was filled with angry, red clouds rolling in memory of yesterday's battle when he throttled a Mexican soldier with bare hands.

During the fateful moment it occurred to McQuillen that his greatest delight would have been to have had his hands on Blake's neck. The idea could not be shaken from his mind. He slowly but unconsciously began to plan to dispose of Blake during battle. He was growing impatient with the wait for the court-martial.

The lean, Texas scout, Williams, clad in a blue shirt, came up and squatted by the campfire to pour himself coffee and ladle beans out of a pot hanging from a crossbar over the fire. He talked while eating. "Taylor's entrenched the wagon train and left a rear guard with four twelve-pound cannons. The Eleventh's been ordered in the lead but it doesn't look like a fight for the Mexes retreated last night leaving a lot of dead and baggage behind!"

"Maybe the general will order a pursuit, eh?" McQuillen said hopefully.

Williams uncoiled himself with exaggerated slowness and faced the sergeant with a half-amused gaze. "Maybe," he smiled softly.

McQuillen left the fire wondering if the scouts were a bunch of fools who believed they knew everything about fighting. All including Zaskq were babes in arms compared with the Seminoles in the Everglades fight.

The army marched at eleven-thirty with the Eleventh in the lead, followed by Ringgold's battery under Ridgeway, since the former's death at Palo Alto. The scouts were set well out as flankers to prevent any surprise attacks from the enemy. But six miles ahead McQuillen suddenly ran into the Mexicans strongly entrenched across the road and retreated hurriedly.

He halted his detail and drew them into the chaparral to await the arrival of the skirmishers, then advanced with them as far as possible along a section of the road called Resaca de la Palma where they engaged the enemy in sharp musketry. But the Mexican firepower was too strong and they were forced back with such rapidity that McQuillen sent the bugler, in haste for reinforcements.

The Eleventh came up fast, but had to halt to let Ridgeway's battery pass, then deployed into skirmishing parties to the left of the road rushing up to the position where McQuillen lay behind a thicket watching the engagement.

The regiment was forced to break into small parties to get through the chaparral. Shortly the Fifth arrived and Captain McCall in temporary command, ordered the scouts forward into the fight. McQuillen hesitated briefly for there were less than a half dozen of the scouts there. He wanted Blake to show up to take responsibility. But after a few moments he decided to move them forward on foot wondering where Blake could be.

His thoughts stayed on the lieutenant during the advance through the brush while grape and canister from the Mexican sixes, nines and ten pieces whipped around his ears. Dropping on hands and knees he crawled rapidly through the underbrush until he reached a break overlooking the position of the Mexican troops.

He saw that the enemy was strongly entrenched in a ravine that crossed the road at a slight bend so he started backwards with intentions of reporting his intelligence. However, on turning he saw Blake starting a charge with an infantry squad, past his position and up the road toward the enemy's guns.

He lifted his rifle and sighted Blake over the barrel. Sheer joy rushed through his big body but then with a whispered curse he dropped his gun as a squad of dragoons flashed between him and his target. They charged into the enemy's batteries to engage themselves in a mass of tangled arms, legs and horses. A fierce death struggle began; the hacking to death of cannoneers while many Americans died impaled on the end of a bloody bayonet.

McQuillen suppressed the violent impulse to leap out of his hiding place and join the murderous fray, but slunk back into the chaparral his eyes glittering. His mind worked with cunning vengeance while watching Blake, joined by the Eleventh, push into the ravine to meet the Mexican troops in a hand-to-hand struggle. It became a fierce, desperate fight in which the Americans knew if defeated there would be no quarters. There was no possibility of retreat and though surrounded by vastly superior numbers they fought with desperation. The Mexican fire was steady and often they used a rest in a fork or a bush. Despite their inferior weapons, they caused havoc among the American troops.

Their guns, which were condemned weapons bought from the British army arsenal, soon started to fail. Then the Americans overran the enemy's position completely routing and chasing them to the neighborhood of Fort Texas where the Mexicans took to the river from all directions, receiving the fire of the eighteen-pounders from the parapet of the fort.

McQuillen never moved from his position but watched the fight keenly. He saw Blake gather the scouts to lead them into a thicket where some of the enemy were still holding out. Simultaneously McQuillen rose and raced low-crouched in a parallel line with the scouts coming in closer behind them.

He flung himself against the ground and crawled rapidly up a small swell to peer over at the scouts fighting in the brush. Blake's back was in his sight, and lifting the musket he sighted and pulled the trigger. Jerking down he realized his shot had missed.

He loaded again, lifted the gun and fired, but Blake turned in time and saw the musket barrel thrust out of the brush. Realizing his danger he threw himself into a ditch as the ball whined over his head. At the same time Warren,

59

with some of the Eleventh, went out into the brush to the left and routed some Mexicans.

McQuillen took advantage of the confusion, flung his rifle aside and raced down the knoll through the thorny brush and came out on the road with the scouts. Warren was pulling Blake out of the ditch as he came up. He avoided Blake's eyes by barking orders at the scouts to round up the prisoners.

The little Indian servant paced the room wringing her hands in anguish. "You can't leave me, Señorita," she moaned. "I'll be murdered in cold blood!"

"You'll be safe at Señor Cordero's house," Sarita replied hurriedly while disrobing. "But be careful in making your way there. The streets are full of drunken soldiers."

She quickly replaced her feminine attire with dark, velvet britches and jacket, put her hair up with pins and combs and pulled on a wide sombrero. She looked like a handsome boy who had just stepped out of a fashion box. Opening a drawer she rummaged around until she found a pepperbox pistol which she loaded and thrust into a side pocket of her cape.

"I am going to the military headquarters to see General Aristo," she said determinedly throwing the cape across her shoulders. "If I do not return in a reasonable time send word to Señor Zaskq."

"Please, Señorita, do not go!" the servant's hands fluttered like helpless birds.

"Perhaps I can appeal to him to stop the crime and debauchery of the Mexican troops against our citizens," she said stepping quickly through the door as the servant's fearful wailing echoed in her ears.

The wild flare of torches lighted the clamoring darkness and the fearful screams of women and shouts of drunken soldiers mingled with the pandemonium. She met mules going the other way loaded with the wounded who bled freely. Their shrieks rose above the uproar and tramp of the retreating army.

She shuddered fearfully for all discipline and order were at an end, and thousands of infuriated Mexican soldiers poured through the streets bent upon rape and plunder. Women fled from the city's ballroom where preparations for a victory celebration were being made, but were submerged in a flood of lawless rancheros who burst upon them in a fury of uncontrolled passion.

Most people had expected an assault on the city by Taylor's troops and had seized a few valuables and fled to the country, but were robbed and murdered on the plains and mountain passes. A bandit chieftain named El Falcon sat outside the city waiting for them.

Sarita slipped through the wild crowd to the edge of town and finally reached the headquarters of the Mexican army. She rode into the camp which was in tumult and confusion from the effort towards a speedy breakup to make a retreat toward Monterrey.

The sentry at the headquarters tent said that General Aristo had already left but one of the staff officers was there, and pulled the curtain flaps aside. As she entered a quick flash of fear rode through her. She recognized Colonel Zapatos, Chief of the Mexican military police. He was a lean, bold eyed man with a sandy beard and reddish hair, dressed in a handsome red and white uniform lavishly decked with gold braid.

His smile changed to a puzzled frown as she stared at him in the lantern light wondering at the arrogance written on his countenance. Then slowly she pulled off her sombrero and shook out her hair. His eyes became bold and bright as recognition took shape in them.

He peered at her closely then said, in a startled whispery voice. "Welcome, Señorita Gonzales!"

61

"Thank you, Colonel," she smiled but was puzzled at his welcome for Zapatos was one of the most ruthless men in all Mexico.

"This is indeed unusual," he bowed slightly. "But I am honored, though it is such a sad occasion. A foe so wily as yourself deserves great honor, or is it that my men are so stupid they let you walk into my tent to kill me!"

"Neither, my dear colonel." she took the chair offered by a barefoot servant. "I've come to make an appeal to you. Please help bring order among your troops. The city is being sacked by our own army, the men murdered and the women and children violated by our troops!"

"Yes, I know," he said taking a glass of wine from the servant. "But what can I do? I've neither a cavalry nor a regiment to quell the disorder!"

She gazed at him in helpless desperation. Why did he say that? Then she noted the cunning expression that flickered across his face like a dark shadow.

"Señorita," he said smoothly. "You would be invaluable to the country of Mexico in helping reorganize the troops. The majority of troops we had for battle were stupid, ignorant peons sent from the haciendas in northern Mexico, who fled at the sound of cannonry. We need fighting men like your Indians to bring glory to Mexico. An appeal from you would bring thousands into the army and you could share in our great victory over the gringos!"

"No, Colonel," she said firmly. "I can't make that kind of an appeal to my people. They don't believe in warfare. I'm pledged to Juquila and it depends upon him!"

"Isn't your word greater than Juquila's?" he asked with disappointment reflecting in his eyes.

"Of course not. It depends entirely on Juquila and you know he is dead set against the present government regime."

"You have influence with him perhaps?" Zapatos asked with inflection in his voice. He was not to be outdone by a slip of a girl.

"None. He makes his own decisions and listens to nobody but the great master Rebazar Tarzs," she became urgent. Would this fool argue all night while people were being murdered in the city streets? "Please do something about the bloodshed going on in the city!"

"You refuse to cooperate with the government?" he asked as his countenance became flushed with rage.

She said furiously. "You would betray our people with further bloodshed? Juquila will hear of this."

"I'll see that Juquila won't hear of this," he said loudly striding to the flaps and called the guard. "Put her under arrest. She will be sent to Mexico City to stand trial for being a traitor to our country!"

Sarita felt a deep frustration welling up as she walked through the darkness with the guard. She wondered about the small pistol hidden under her hat. Could she use it in escaping? Perhaps. She knew the military caste intended to betray her people and prolong the war under the pretense of victory. Her people would never win a war under the present regime. The country was overrun by revolutionists and dictators, especially Santa Anna, until there was little fight left in the citizens, and no money in the national treasury. If they lost another battle France and England might step in for colonial conquests.

They reached a dark spot where several horses stood. The sentry told her to mount. She swung into the saddle, reaching for the pistol under her hat. Turning to point it at the sentry she found herself staring into Peddar Zaskq's face.

He spoke in a low voice and the sentry dropped his gun. He quickly bound and gagged him. Then mounting he silently motioned for her to follow and rode off swiftly into the night.

They skirted the city coming out on the south side where looking back they saw fires lighting the horizon and heard the screams of men in the distance. The moon was over the hills now, casting its beautiful light across the plains and burning city.

63

Pausing, the scout turned in the saddle. "I had word that you had gone to Aristo. It is well that I came to find you."

"He was sending me to Monterrey where Ampudia would make arrangements for my transportation to Mexico City to stand trial. What are you going to do with me?"

Peddar Zaskq chuckled softly. "Take you to Monterrey but not in bonds. We will find an escort down the road. Let's hurry."

Within a few moments of riding they saw horsemen approaching in the moonlight and pulled off into the shadows. As the riders passed she noticed a tall, gaunt American officer with a blonde girl whose hair was braided down her back, and a huge man in a red jacket with a high shako. Behind them was another American, a powerful, brutal faced man, who sat like a bull on his horse.

Zaskq raised his hand to hail them, but dark riders swept in from the darkness beyond seizing the girl. He fired at them yelling for the Americans. In a few moments they had recaptured the girl and drove off the attackers who fled in the night.

Peddar Zaskq said, "Thank You. You have rescued my dear friend, Sarita Gonzales." Turning to her he continued. "These are my officers in the Yankee army, Lieutenant Blake . . . "

Sarita felt the eyes of the American officer sweep over her. They were the clear yellow eyes of a man she knew would come to know her well. Major Dennis glanced at her briefly for he was fatigued and dejected. He had been rescued from prison at Matamoros. The sergeant showed something deeply coarse in his features; a man to be feared. The red scar under his right eye twitched.

"I am taking her away, Lieutenant," Zaskq said gravely. "There has been trouble for her. I want to take her to safety. Could I have a two day pass?"

Blake nodded wishing them a safe journey. They galloped away in the moonlight with the Mexican girl feeling a strange throb within herself from the glance which passed between herself and the American Lieutenant.

She wondered if it would be he who would fulfill the prophecy of her destiny. Was he the white warrior from the north who was to come into her life?

She shook the thought out of her head and let the reins out on the horse as they thundered into the whole moonlight across the plains. The dark, mysterious shadows lay heavy across the hills. From somewhere there came the soft beating of drums. The drums of ECK.

Chapter Five

Brigadier General Zachary Taylor studied the report on his table with meticulous care. It was a recommendation for a court-martial for Lieutenant Jed Blake, Chief of Scouts for the Eleventh Regiment. He was not pleased with the finding of the report.

He finished and while trying to form an opinion drank from a mug of coffee. His keen blue eyes gazed through the slit in the curtain flaps at the distant horizon of mountains. After awhile he turned and spoke to the officer sitting at the far side of the tent, "What's your opinion, Bill? Should I hold a court on Blake?"

"I'd advise against it, General," replied his tall, handsome son-in-law. "There's danger in a court-martial of this kind in a field campaign. It hurts the morale of the officers. You know that striking an enlisted man isn't too serious a charge during an invasion expedition. We can ruin a good officer quickly, and Blake has the making of one."

"I don't like the word invasion. That's the West Point talking through you." The general tapped his fingers brusquely on the desk and started to speak, but checked himself for he valued the advice of Bliss.

"Lieutenant Don Carlos Buell hit one of his men with a saber at Palo Alto and got off with a reprimand."

Taylor tapped the desk harder. He could never reach a satisfactory understanding with his son-in-law. "Buell hit a private, not a sergeant," he snapped. "And it was Hitchcock who recommended the punishment."

"Blake's got the best military background of any the young officers in service except Kirby-Smith. He comes from a good fighting stock."

"Tradition! Bah!" Taylor snorted. "We don't fight battles with family reputations, Bill. The Seminoles didn't stop to examine Blake's pedigree at Lake Royal!"

Bliss smiled. "I'll remind you that Blake's father was one of Scott's best friends. His family has a great military record which gives him a degree of respectability. However, it's entirely your decision, General!"

Taylor gave his companion a sharp glance but realized he had better not speak his mind for he was fortunate to have Bliss appointed to his staff as headquarters adjutant. Bliss knew the etiquette for military procedure and was able to keep matters straight between himself and the War Department. He was an invaluable man.

His thoughts were wrapped around his military planning. He had twice whipped the Mexicans in battle and the next movement was to proceed up the Rio Grande to Camargo and then to Monterrey, a walled city and capital of the Department of Nuevo Leon. From there he would move his troops to the mountain town of Saltillo and from this strongly posted position he could control northern Mexico.

The odds against him made him smile. General Winfield Scott, Chief of Staff, was trying to undermine him with the President and the administration. There were hardly enough regulars in the field to fight a decent battle. The victories at Palo Alto and Resaca de la Palma were won by Ringgold's excellent artillery. Ringgold was the top artillery officer in the service and had trained his department to be the highest and most efficient, but he was dead. Who would take the place of this man who would be called the father of American artillery?

Scott didn't like him. The old commander-in-chief refused to send him the best regulars and most of the volunteers

68

were raggle-tailed street bums. Scott thought him an incompetent fool who knew nothing about modern warfare.

He continued to think and smile. His years in frontier fighting began to tell on his health. Now sixty, he was not able to stand the hardships as during the years in the Indian wars. Still he had greater stamina and could campaign with the best of his officers. West Point should send him real men instead of the lily whites which had been coming during this campaign. Why they weren't even saddle-hardened.

"All right, Bill," he said testily. "I'll drop the court-martial and give Blake a reprimand. I still don't like it for no officer should strike an enlisted man!"

Bliss said cautiously. "I agree with you, sir!"

Taylor spoke again, "I might as well do it now as any other time. Fetch Blake here at once!"

While waiting the old general let his memories drift back to his youthful days in Kentucky. He joined the army before he was twenty and became an officer at twenty-two. He didn't understand an officer who hit his own men regardless of the provocation. Rumors came to him about Blake being in hot water over the death of his younger brother. It wasn't a pretty story but after all there was nothing gentle about war. The army was tough and the things told about the troops were hardly fit for the ears of gentle folks.

The court martial of Major Dennis, after his release from the Mexican prison, had a deep effect on the officers of his army. Taylor was thinking he didn't want to repeat the same mistake twice, but Blake's case warranted stern action; however, against his better judgment he had let Bliss sway him.

Something queer about this case. Calloway had been acting strange for weeks and looked as though he had something besides his daughter's presence on his mind. Taylor wondered if it would have anything to do with the mixup of orders at Lake Royal. Calloway had never gotten over that and had been playing granddaddy to Blake ever since.

69

He knew Calloway was in bad shape. The colonel had given his whole life to the service but he had the worst possible breaks. Passed over in his promotions to full colonelcy he had become morose and unhappy with the army. Scott didn't like Calloway and had done everything possible to make service life miserable for him and since the Lake Royal fiasco seriously undermined him.

Blake's arrival broke the chain of thought. Turning, he looked at the slim officer standing there. "At ease, Lieutenant," he said gruffly while studying Blake with hard eyes. "There is a bad report on you, Lieutenant. Anything you want to say in self-defense?"

"Nothing, sir," Blake's yellow eyes were fixed in a steady gaze on the general's face.

"I've decided against a court, Blake," Taylor said swinging around and locking gazes with Blake. He was thinking that the young officer was taking this with courage and resolution. "You can thank Captain Bliss for that. But I don't like this report of you striking your sergeant. Nobody hits sergeants in my army. Haven't you been told that before?"

"Yes, sir," Blake replied calmly.

"You must have had a good reason," Taylor continued roughly exasperated at Blake's calmness. "Want to tell me about it?"

"It was a personal matter, sir."

"Was it over that report about your brother's death?" Taylor asked shrewdly watching Blake's face and saw the tiniest flicker break the calm mask for only a fraction of a second.

"Yes, sir," Blake said flatly.

Taylor half turned in his chair but kept his keen gaze on the young officer. "Do you think it's about time to send Calloway's daughter back to the states?" he asked.

"She didn't have anything to do with it," Blake replied.

Taylor suddenly glared at the officer for his trap went awry. He caught his son-in-law's eye and saw him shake his

70

head in warning. Angrily, Taylor swallowed his pride. "We'll leave it this way, Blake. But I'm putting the incident on your record as a reprimand and sending a full report to Washington. You may be passed over for your next promotion."

His voice went hard. "That's all Lieutenant. If this happens again I'll see that you're drummed out of service!"

He got up and faced his adjutant. Before Blake had reached the tent flaps he gave an abrupt order. "Get the troops ready to march at once," he said bluntly. "We've got a lot of ground to cover before reaching Monterrey!"

Sweaty, smelling horses and the creak of saddles made up the world of Lieutenant Jed Blake as the scouts rode into the open plains passing a company of dragoons under Major Dennis who acknowledged his salute with a curt nod.

Blake felt a slow stirring of his temper but got control of himself. Dennis was arrogant and angry despite the fact that Fortune and he, with a detail of scouts, rescued the Major and other American prisoners from a Mexican jail filled with crawling vermin and filth.

Dennis had received a court-martial and had been punished with loss of pay for his conduct in leaving the base without permission with Thornton's troops which had been captured by the Mexicans before the last two battles had taken place. Even though the punishment was light it was a thorn in Dennis' side after he had gone to so much trouble to get Blake before a court. However, Blake was puzzled by Fortune's turn of attitude for she was now constantly seen with Dennis.

His thoughts drifted back to the reprimand by Taylor. It was discouraging to have another black mark on his record, after an apparently good beginning in the service. McQuillen had been responsible for both of them, one in

Florida and the other in Mexico.

He became conscious of the world around him. The sun was a fierce lance, a saber, a spear, a burning flame that beat against his head and into the deep recesses of his brain. He rode with his head bent forward and his eyes closed to a slit, against the glare of the sun, watching the remote outline of the roan's hooves moving slowly one after another, against the parched earth.

Raising his head Blake saw that they were more than a half mile south of Matamoros, and ordered the scouts to fan out in wide flankers. Half-turning in his saddle he gave a cursory glance down the line of scouts as if gathering muster. Corporal Harry Michael, a bold faced man with thick whiskers and a cheerful attitude, rode behind McQuillen. The scout was chuckling softly to himself as if his memory had served up something humorous for his mind to chew up.

Blake's glance took in the rest of the scouts. They were dressed in rough blues with forage caps, pistols stuck in belted waists with Bowie knives and short carbine rifles in saddle holsters.

He identified them in his mind. There were Privates Titus Hultkrans, a Swede from the Tennessee mountains; Sam Campbell, once a wealthy playboy from Boston; Virgil Bush from Chicago; Julius Ichler, a Jew from southern Illinois; Rueben Arnold, an army veteran and corporal; Jack Burkhart, a kid seeking adventure; Osborne, a Missouri farmhand; Williams and Peddar Zaskq who had just returned from escorting the Mexican woman to safety. Twelve in all, they were.

He stopped his observation and sent Williams and Zaskq forward on a patrol then resumed his thinking about the scouts again. The scouts had been with him for months, all except Williams and Zaskq, who joined at Corpus Christi. He had lived with the others since the day he received orders at New Orleans to proceed to St. Joseph Island with the Eleventh for reassignment in the field.

Each scout was an individual problem but he knew they had a common goal, all except Williams and Peddar Zaskq. That goal was to get enough loot out of Mexico to live in indolent ease the rest of their lives. He had little illusion about this gang of cutthroats and thieves assigned to his command.

On the other hand the general opinion was that Taylor had changed his mind about the fighting ability of the West Pointers. He had told the younger officers including Hardee, Grant, Meade, Porter, Bragg, Jackson, Hooker, Doubleday, Casey, Mansfield, Buell, Longstreet, Hill, Johnson and other West Pointers after the last battle that they had become veterans worthy of the army's respect.

Now Taylor was moving his troops forward. He had ordered a mixed command of volunteers and regulars to Reynosa and Camargo, some few miles up the Rio Grande. The Eleventh had not yet moved so Blake with the rest of the troops awaited the arrival of Major Belton with additional companies of artillery. With the new arrivals the army would have a regular force of more than three thousand regulars and ten thousand volunteers in the field.

Deep within himself Blake began to feel the steady drumming. Nervously he looked around wondering what it meant. Was it the prelude to some violence? The sound occurred when there was danger. His annoyance was suddenly broken by gunfire and Williams appeared from out of the brush lashing his horse in a hard run.

Blake jerked his roan to an abrupt halt, signaling the scouts, and whipped the telescope from his saddlebag to study the landscape. He found nothing of an ominous nature to greet this searching glance. The dry, sandy world was a bleached prism of sunlight reflected in some forbidden way. Puzzled he waited for the rider who came abreast and pulled up in a cloud of dust.

Williams cried, "Zaskq has been taken prisoner by the dragoons. They accused him of being a hostile!"

"Lead the way!" Blake shouted.

Anger flared through him as he dug spurs into the roan's flanks and thundered recklessly through the chaparral where cactus thorns ripped their uniforms. Williams broke through a thicket into a glade where a half dozen dragoons were gathered around Zaskq who was astride his horse, hands tied and a rope around his neck. The loose end was flung over a tree limb and held taut by a trooper.

Blake pulled up in the midst of the dragoons, facing Dennis. His first thoughts were that Dennis was seeking revenge but the officer's face was a dull reddish flush and his eyes were glazed. He had been drinking.

"What's this?" Blake demanded flipping the rope off Zaskq's neck.

Dennis spoke in a whiskey voice. "This scoundrel was caught riding near our dragoons. He can't identify himself; Looks like a spic to me!"

"He is my guide!"

"How was I to believe him?" Dennis snarled. "He's too dark to be a white man. I thought he was a spic."

"With those blue eyes?" Blake said evenly with pursed lips. "If you hurt this man, you'll answer to Colonel Calloway!"

Their eyes met in a hot glare, then Dennis motioned for his dragoons to release the guide. "All right Blake. He's your responsibility."

After Dennis and his troops had disappeared in the brush, Blake demanded, "Where's your pass?"

Zaskq half-smiled. "It was in my pants pocket before I went to sleep last night."

"Somebody steal it?" he asked.

"I've an idea who stole it, but how can I prove it?" Zaskq said.

"I think so too," Blake replied dryly, kicking his horse into action. "Let's get along and get the bugler to call in the scouts."

"Are you in love with the fair-skinned warrior from the north?" asked the muscular, six foot dark brown man clad in a maroon robe and barefooted, sitting opposite Sarita. He had deep shining black eyes that expressed dark fire within himself.

The girl gave him a quick glance. "No," she laughed. "I hardly know him, yet I do think of him often."

His black eyes were coals of shining fire, his lips were purple and his speech a clipped style as he almost barked his words. "You must use every possible caution since Santa Anna has returned to Mexico. He has taken over the government and is seeking out his old enemies. His specific promises of peace completely gulled the Americano president, for he knew our countrymen too well to imagine any Mexican government staying in power should he refuse to fight an invader. Besides, there is no other Mexican as capable as he in raising and organizing armies in such a short time."

"What brings you to Monterrey, Sire?" she asked knowing he would not answer any question about the prophecy of the white warrior from the north.

"To warn you personally," he said rising to his feet to leave. The girl was dear to him and he could not let her make sacrifices but the mission must be fulfilled. "Forget the Yankee officer and think of the duty which is before you."

"The memory of meeting him that night at Matamoros stays with me," she admitted flushing.

"Drop him from your mind," Rebazar Tarzs said. "It takes your attention from your duties and endangers your life. Santa Anna has learned of your political activities and offers a ten thousand pesos reward for your capture alive."

"I know," she said. "Zapatos almost caught me in Matamoros, through my own stupidity. Should I stay here or leave?"

"You cannot leave here yet. But be not afraid even though they capture you. You have the pellet of poison which is to be taken whenever torture is started on you."

"Must you leave?" she asked as he turned. "It is so lonely when I cannot see you."

"Duty calls in other parts of this poor country. You will stay here and attend to my desires."

"Yes, Sire," she promised.

"You will always live a hazardous life, Sarita. This was written in the stars at your birth," he paused looking through the window at the broad sweep of land to the beautiful walnut grove where lay the camp of the Gringo army. "The battle for the city of Monterrey will soon begin. I am certain that it will be bloody and costly to the city, and your life will be in great peril. Do not falter but keep faith with those who work for peace. When the last shot is fired, go across the battlefield with water, bandages, medicines and stretchers to look after the sick, wounded and dead of both sides.

"You are to help organize the city government after the battle. Get the people back to work as quickly as possible and see that life is resumed again, as before. Never mind about the dangers it puts you in. Be above fear and yourself to serve the people. This is your destiny O daughter of the Sun!"

He put his hand gently on her shoulder. A deep feeling of emotion ran through her, centering at her heart. "And may my love always be with you," he spoke abruptly.

His deep voice reached into the very core of her brain, winding around her thoughts, shaking her to the roots of herself. "If I could only stay with you," she murmured.

"We will be together again when The SUGMAD instructs it to be," his deep voice answered. "But if you hear the drums of ECK calling return at once!"

For a long time after he was gone she stood at the window watching the smoke curl upward through the trees around the gringo camp. Her mind was whirling so rapidly she could hardly think. Then she went over to the bed and lay down calling for her servant to bring a cup of chocolate.

An age-old emotion began to rise in her. She thought about the American officer that night in Matamoros. To love a man other than her master Rebazar Tarzs, or Juquila — to give herself completely, her body and soul, was something she did not desire to do. Yet she trembled with the thought. A previous experience in her life caused her to shrink from this and seek the fulfillment of her happiness in the SUGMAD. She had many admirers and suitors but only the attainment of love for the SUGMAD was self-satisfying.

The roar of gunfire brought General Zachary Taylor out of a light sleep at dawn, September 21, 1846, in a rush to the curtains of the tent, shouting for his aide.

He had dozed off in his chair after an all night vigil at his table while studying the battle strategy and writing orders in anticipation of an assault on Monterrey. The lantern light was fading out in the early morning mist, and he peered through the curtains with blurred eyes and hair tousled. To his surprise he was alone, neither his guard nor orderly were about. He let out a roar for his adjutant.

When Captain Bliss appeared, Taylor shouted, "What's the racket about?"

"Worth must be under attack, sir," Bliss replied tactfully. "Sounds as if it's coming from the south side of the city where he took up position last night."

"Quit sirring me and get the facts," Taylor fumed picking up a mug of cold coffee, drained it but spit it out quickly. "And get back here fast for orders!"

While the adjutant was gone Taylor washed, shaved and put on a clean shirt keeping his attention riveted to the distant firing. A mess boy arrived with breakfast and a pot of coffee, but Taylor took only coffee, sat down and quickly went through the orders he had spent the night writing.

Captain Bliss returned shortly with a report that Worth's division was advancing on the enemy, and the Texas Rangers, in the division, were under attack by a body of some thousand Mexican lancers. The attack lasted briefly after the enemy's commanding officer was killed.

Taylor directed Bliss to have the battery on the lower side of the city commence firing, and for General Garland's brigade to make a demonstration before the city to draw the Mexicans' fire. He left the tent, mounted old Whitey and rode to the edge of camp where he watched the action through his telescope. Garland's brigade had moved to the city limits where it had been stalled by a murderous crossfire.

Twiggs seeing the difficulty made a spirited assault up one street intending to turn the foe's flank and attack the first fort from the rear, but was trapped in a similar situation. His men were exposed to musket fire from the fort and a lone battery which swept them with grapeshot. Confusion was added by fire from at least a thousand muskets from the rooftops.

The pageantry of colors, the swirling flags and roar of battle stirred Taylor tremendously. This was Tippecanoe again. Who said he was incapable of modern warfare? Old Scott, Gaines and the rest of his critics should see this.

Suddenly he thought of Blake, and wondered why he should think of the young officer in midst of battle. He dismissed the thought and shouted at his aide to order Colonel Jefferson Davis to bring up his regiment of Mississippians. A few minutes later Davis, his other son-in-law, rode by on Pompey, an iron-gray war-horse, at the head of his Mississippi riflemen and the Tennessee Volunteers.

As they approached the swirling battle Colonel Davis rose in his stirrups and gallantly waved his sword. "We can take that fort with knives if you've got the courage!" he yelled above the roar of gunfire.

Yelling at every step his troops swarmed to the relief of Twiggs' brigade. They waded through a baptism of heavy fire, scaling the walls of the fort despite heavy losses, pouring into the fort so rapidly the Mexicans were disorganized and their officers captured.

Turning his attention to the right Taylor saw the First Ohio Volunteers, led by the young West Pointers, Joe Hooker, Daniel Harvey Hill, and Albert Sidney Johnston, storm the streets of the city where a sheet of firepower from the enemy guns drove them back. Taylor put spurs to old Whitey dashing to the head of the Ohio regiment. Dismounting he grabbed a pickaxe shouting for the troops to follow.

A wild scream arose from the throats of the Americans as they surged forward behind Taylor, knocking in doors. They pushed into the houses and rushed to the rooftops to clean off the Mexican sharpshooters whose murderous musketry fire had been so costly to the Yankees.

Captain Braxton Bragg brought up his battery of light artillery in full gallop to Garland's brigade which was bogged down in the cornfield. A company of Mexican lancers furiously charged from the Black Fort but the firepower of the Americans drove them back. They retreated and formed again with almost a thousand horsemen in reinforcements. By this time Bragg's battery had gotten into position in the cornfield and when the Mexican lancers appeared again, opened heavy fire. The horsemen retreated in confusion back into the city.

By evening the captured fort and its vicinity was strongly entrenched with American troops. The other regiments were ordered back to camp. Dead and wounded men covered the plains under the range of the Black Fort's guns. Bodies of American soldiers were scattered over the cornfields at the edge of the city, and in the streets where Garland's troops were so badly cut to pieces. The troops who fell into the hands of the Mexicans were slaughtered or barbarously mangled and stripped of their clothing.

Blake was glad to see the battle halted. He had been on the west side of the city where Worth's division captured the Mexican fortifications on the lofty ridges while on the far side of the river a fort was stormed and captured by four hundred men which included Calloway's regiment.

They remained in possession of the fort on the heights that night, sleeping on their arms. At dawn orders were given to the troops to storm the enemy's heights nearest the Saltillo road. Blake and his scouts prepared for the battle while the strange drums beat in his brain. They joined the troops under Worth storming the heights that were half-hidden in a gray fog rolling across the lofty heights. The Mexicans' fire was light as they hurriedly retreated across to the next fort, called the Bishop's Fort.

The Americans were ordered to hold their positions and get ready for an attempt on the Bishop's Fort. The movement looked like a tough assignment but the main body of Americans were concealed from the Mexicans by a crest of ridges above, and were in position to fire down upon the enemy. Four companies were cut out of the division and deployed to make an attack on the Mexican's flank. Blake and his scouts were sent ahead to lead the attack.

As they set out in formation for the assault Blake saw the lovely, dark-skinned girl, Sarita Gonzales, crossing the summit, on horseback. She dismounted beside a wounded soldier, and hailed a passing native trooper to help place him across the rump of her horse. Riding off she saw Blake and paused to look down at him. He lifted his hand and waved, but she did not return his hail.

Disappointed, Blake ordered his men to advance up the hill. They struggled over the rocky ground, sheltering themselves behind boulders while heavy musket and cannon fire kept them pinned against the earth.

He received word to get ready for the assault for the softening up process was taking place. Captain Robert E. Lee, an army engineer, using mules had pulled a twelve-pounder howitzer up the heights and placed it in position to fire into the fort. The howitzer was fired with such deadly effect that the Mexicans sallied forth to charge the heights. Blake's scouts caught the full impact of the charge and were overrun. They retreated to the main body of troops who came up fast and dislodged the enemy.

The Mexicans were driven back into the fort where they poured a murderous fire into the ranks of the advancing Americans, but the Yanks moved against the fortifications spreading their lines in order to break the concentration of the enemy's firepower.

Blake felt the fury of the attack as men fell around him like leaves in an autumn gale. They were suddenly upon the fort in a mad, desperate rush, screaming like crazy men. Arnold with a bloody handkerchief tied around his head, drove his bayonet through a Mexican lifting him like a bale of hay.

McQuillen entered the fray wielding a big knife and his pistol and wearing an ugly, dangerous look on his scarred face. Blake glanced down the line at his scouts to see them in a bloody rush murdering the helpless foe. His stomach revolted, but he gained satisfaction on discovering that Peddar Zaskq was absent.

The fortress was captured and the rest of the Mexicans fled into the city where with reinforcements they started setting up another line of defense. Throughout the rest of the day there was little infantry action, but the cannoning continued. The next morning the battle was resumed with fury against the Mexican army which had withdrawn into the city to the Plaza where a determined stand could be made on the rooftops.

General Quitman's brigade, supported by Garland's regulars, entered the east side of the city, while Worth attacked the western half, moving into a cemetery where his men planted a mortar and started throwing shells into the plaza. The fire created havoc among the enemy troops and they started a stampede like frightened animals. The Americans split into small detachments of fifty or sixty men and drove into the city over roofs and through houses.

Quitman's men fought their way doggedly up the open street while being raked by grapeshot and swept by fire from swarms of snipers on sandbagged roofs. Their ammunition ran out within a block of the plaza and Lieutenant U.S. Grant, of the Fourth Infantry, volunteered to ride back to bring up more. Hanging over the side of his horse, like an Indian, Grant galloped through the city with Mexicans firing at him from every street corner. Instead of sending the ammunition, Taylor ordered Quitman to withdraw and postponed all operations until morning.

The enemy was reduced to a small section around the plaza by nightfall, which on Thursday morning tried to defend itself against the onslaughts of the Americans. But the destruction and carnage was so great that General Ampudia, commander of the Mexican army, surrendered to Taylor with the agreement that he could retreat to Linares with his army and full equipment, including the Mexican artillery.

Blake was so relieved to find the opportunity to lie down again and rest although his mind was stunned by the catastrophe which his own people had created. He wondered about Sarita Gonzales. Was she lying dead among the ruins of the city walls? His mind would not stop whirling with worry.

Then the drums started again!

Chapter Six

Jed Blake rose from his sleeping blankets and fumbled for boots in the darkness. The restlessness which had disturbed his sleep most of the evening drove him from the tent. The night was raw and chilly, and the blazing stars in the dark sky were so close he felt that his hands could almost reach up and touch them.

His mind was in an awful confused state and his nervous system upset from the effects of the terrible ordeal of the battle. His hands shook while trying to light his pipe and pulling steadily on the heavy stem he watched the stars. The smoke in his throat seemed to clear his brain.

Like the rest of the men in the army Blake was low in spirit, but should have been otherwise from their splendid victory. General Taylor openly admitted that his army was reduced to its lowest strength, for the Texas troops had been discharged and sent home. To replace them Taylor had counted on the arrival of the Tennessee and Kentucky mounted infantry regiments, but they had been routed by San Antonio and would be a long time reaching the front. The army's strength was further dwindled by chills, fever, dysentery and other diseases, besides the bands of Mexican robbers who hung upon the American lines to rob and kill.

The army's morale was so low that the Irish Catholics, influenced by the church propaganda, were deserting in wholesale lots. Riley, former gunner in the Fourth Regiment, was blamed for many desertions. He had abandoned the army at Matamoros and fought against his former comrades during the last three days. When the Mexicans left the city, under truce terms, he rode out with the artillery jeering at his former friends in the American army.

The chilled night air seemed to twist his thoughts into strange patterns. This was a new world to him, this strange mysterious Mexico with it's high mountains looming down on this sturdy little American army, and the conquered city.

This land was surely ruled by the ancient gods of Mexico. He shook his head angrily to get the thoughts out of his mind. This was pagan talk like Peddar Zaskq would give out. Was he, Lieutenant Jed Blake, USA, a civilized person, going to let heathenism replace his principles of religious beliefs?

He walked across to the campfire, seated himself on a log and stared into the flickering flames with his thoughts on Sarita Gonzales. Why was he thinking about the Mexican girl at this time? She had seen him on the mountain ridge at Monterrey and ignored his hail. Did she hate him because he was an American, and had she sent her brother to spy on the Yankee army?

Somebody approached on light, steady steps, from beyond the circle of firelight. He rose quickly with one hand on his pistol, but relaxed as Peddar Zaskq stepped into the ring of light.

The scout eyed him narrowly. "You cannot sleep, Captain?" he asked.

"I can't sleep," Blake replied gruffly seating himself again. He wondered what to say to his guide. He couldn't come out abruptly and ask about Sarita. Did he want to reveal himself now?

The man sat down on the other end of the log, a slim, dark figure in tight, blue buckskins, velvet jacket and short cap. "The SUGMAD will not let you sleep tonight," he said.

84

"Who are you, Zaskq? What are you doing with the American army?" There was a hard note in Blake's voice.

"I'm only an instrument of God, Captain," his smooth features wrinkled in a smile. "It is my desire to help this country to be restored to order and peace again. Since war has come with the United States, then it must be war. Who am I to say what the will of The SUGMAD shall be?"

"I once lived with the Mayans whose ancient civilization has never been surpassed by any other race on this planet. Our great teacher is the ancient god, The SUGMAD, and one of my ancestors was ITS personal disciple. The teachings have been handed down from father to son. But I was taught by the great Rebazar Tarzs."

"Just what do you believe?" Blake asked mockingly, half-annoyed that he had to listen to some lecture on paganism.

"We believe the Mahanta is the ancient one, the son of God, that he came from the SUGMAD. We believe that this same God who keeps the earth in its path must also keep the other worlds in their paths. But, this truth is as I know it, my friend. Rebazar Tarzs taught me there is one God regardless of whether he is your Christian God or the Mexican God. We only worship him differently."

Blake studied the scout curiously. Dressed in blue clothing he was a strange one. Zaskq was a paradox to Blake, a man of peace, but always ready to defend himself and others against unnecessary violence.

Superstition and nonsense he thought, but nevertheless he knew that the scout was serious. Hoping to sidetrack the subject Blake said, "I have wondered about your friend Señorita Gonzales. Isn't it dangerous for her to be following the Mexican army hoping to get them to cease fighting?"

Peddar Zaskq smiled sadly and pulled a serape around his shoulders. "My friend is accustomed to danger," he said. "She is a very capable person, indeed, and I am proud of her."

"She is very beautiful," Blake murmured gazing at the leaping flames.

"Ah, yes, Captain," the scout replied. "But she has lived a sad and proud life. Her desire is great for God, like that of the stars which will not let the clouds hide them in the midnight sky. Yet her beauty is fatal to anyone who seeks her hand.

"Yes, she has had many suitors, but she has been so unattainable that duels have been fought over her honor and some killed for the least slur breathed upon her name. Three of the finest young men in all Mexico blew out their brains after her refusal of marriage. Men seem to warm their hearts by her beauty but do violent things to one another to be the first in line for her favor!"

Blake felt a sting of jealousy. "She cares for no man?" he asked in amazement.

"For nothing but the SUGMAD," the scout said softly. "She is very humble to God. But there was one poor devil, a German, a soldier of fortune, who came to Mexico a few years ago and fell in love with her. She believed it was the fulfillment of a childhood prophecy which said she was going to marry a white warrior from the north. A terrible thing happened."

His voice ended in a deadly whisper and something awful flowed out from Zaskq like a force striking Blake with its invisible violence. Briefly, there was no sound except for the soft utterable note of a mockingbird in a lonely mogote and the mountain breeze blowing emptily through the grass. Far away at the foot of the mountain a pack of coyotes were snarling over something—probably the bones of a Yankee soldier.

Slowly turning his head Blake found the man's eyes bent upon him with a harrowed gaze that gleamed like blue diamonds. The change in the man's countenance shook him, made a cold shiver run up his spinal column.

"What happened?" Blake asked in a low voice.

"He thought she was pagan and took advantage of her love," the scout replied rising to his feet with one hand. "And he bragged about it!"

The flickering firelight showed the terrible drawn lines as he stared at Blake. Behind him was the background of the night in a lost world. The flames leaped higher.

He spoke in a husky whisper. "Death was a pleasure to him after her family finished with him."

He stepped backwards and was instantly lost in that terrible blackness of the night. Somewhere under the dark sky the coyotes were howling like lost souls.

"We oughta have a little fun sometime," Hultkrans muttered as he stepped cautiously along the narrow, high-walled street with Campbell and Ichler following.

Darkness closed in around them as they moved toward the post office building in the center of the city where a number of American soldiers met secretly each night to gossip and gamble. Occasionally they halted and hid in the shadow as a sentry passed, then continued on their journey.

"I don't like this," Ichler said glancing about fearfully. His hooked nose made him look like a buccaneer. "We oughtn't to have come alone!"

"What you scared about?" Campbell asked slouching along in the rear.

"Mexes. They can throw a knife in the dark!"

Hultkrans said, "Ain't nothing gonna hurt you!"

"All the same I wish we'd stayed in camp and played cards with the rest of the fellers," Ichler growled. "What we doin' here anyway?"

"That's as plain as the beak on your puss," Campbell chuckled softly. "Old Taylor won't let us gamble in camp."

Taylor's victory at Monterrey seemed hollow for the troops for he made the groggeries and gambling houses off limits to them. Even the Mexican army had marched out of the city after surrendering, its bands playing, flags flying and the city population cheering. The troops were to join Santa Anna at San Luis Potosí, three hundred miles to the south where the greatest force of Mexicans ever seen in that country were being concentrated.

Polk showed his displeasure by canceling the armistice and sent more volunteers to Mexico. The new troops poured into camp, overran the little army, ate up its food supply, took over the equipment and did nothing but create trouble. He used reports from Taylor's enemies in the field about waste and inefficiency in the army as an excuse to send Brigadier General Robert Patterson, a lifelong friend and Democrat to take charge of the Volunteers and occupy Tamaulipas.

The three scouts turned a corner and stopped abruptly in the narrow street almost falling over one another. The rising moon threw its light across the cobblestones to reveal the figures of five Mexicans standing there with raised guns.

"Buenas noches, amigos," one of them grinned with white gleaming teeth.

"What are we going to do?" Ichler whispered fearfully.

Hultkrans exclaimed hoarsely. "Stay together. Don't shoot unless they rush us. follow me!"

They wheeled to retreat down the narrow street but two more Mexicans in sloppy sombreros blocked their escape from behind. Hultkrans let out a hissing breath and motioned for his companions to back against the street wall. The Mexicans moved toward them with moonlight gleaming on musket barrels.

"Get ready!" Hultkrans grunted with sweat rolling off his hot face. "When I say shoot, pull the triggers. I'll have at least a dead one before they get me!"

Just then a tall, rawboned man stepped around the corner and barked a sharp order in Spanish. The Mexicans halted, turned and argued fluently with the tall man who replied with savage curses. They withdrew as silently as they appeared.

The man turned to the scouts. "Howdy, boys," he drawled. "Remember me?"

"I sure do,"Hultkrans growled. "It's Tom Riley! Thought you rode out with the Mexican artillery the other day."

Riley squatted in the street, a long pattern of shadows against the cobblestones. "Now don't take that attitude, boys," he grinned. "I'm not really a traitor, but doing the army a favor. You might call it spying or such!"

"Like crazy," Campbell retorted bitterly. "The Mexes pay you more cash than the army. That's why you deserted!"

Hultkrans dropped on his haunches beside Riley. "Don't pay him no mind, Tom. He ain't appreciative of you saving our lives!"

"Yeah, I know," Riley grinned. "But what are you boys doing in this ungodly place at this hour?"

"We're headed for the old post office building. There's a game going on there. Like to join us?"

Riley shook his head. "Some of them guys might be like Sam. Want to shoot me. I'm in town for business. That was some of my boys who was gonna shoot your livers to pieces. I'm a Captain now, fellers. The Mexes are treating all Americans who desert to our side pretty good!"

"I'll be!" Ichler ejaculated. "Maybe this desertin' stuff ain't so bad after all!"

"It's all right fellers, but there's something bigger in the wind than deserting. You can make yourselves a pretty good chunk of dough!"

"How's that?" Hultkrans cried.

"This is secret stuff," Riley said cautiously looking at Campbell who was sulking in the background. "What about him?"

"I'm always interested in cash," Campbell said quickly.

"This is about a big spy ring working in these parts. The Mexes have been wanting to break it up for a long time.

89

They've got a price on the heads of any leaders caught and turned over to them alive. Some of them are in your army operating for the Yanks."

"How'd we know who they might be, Tom?" Campbell asked attentively.

"You won't know until I tell you," Riley grinned. "They are all members of a gang operating under the guise of religion. Claim to be followers of a God called The SUGMAD. There's ten thousand pesos reward for the leaders. We'll split fifty-fifty."

"Sixty-forty," Hultkrans growled.

"Sure if you want it that way," Riley got to his feet. "Hafta go now, fellers. I'll tip you off if any news comes my way."

"Hey!" Campbell said. "Who is that leader in our army?"

"Now I can't rightly say I know," Riley laughed easily. But I'll give you a real good tip. Keep your eyes peeled on that scout Peddar Zaskq. His girlfriend is mixed up in this deal, too, and while you're watching the Mex, you might keep an eye on that Lieutenant Blake. Hearing things about him too!"

Blake was seated on his mess chest in his quarters reading a letter from his mother, dated the middle of October. It was a little over three weeks in reaching him at Saltillo where the First Division, under Worth, had been moved from Monterrey.

Her letter said that Polk realizing the military weakness of the army scattered over northern Mexico now turned his attention toward the invasion of Vera Cruz. Swift, hard blows had to be struck to end the war for it was no longer popular in the states with Daniel Webster of New Hampshire leading a congressional fight against Polk's administration.

90

Blake put down the letter thinking about the invasion talk that spread through the army. Many thought Taylor would strike south into the heart of Mexico or at Tampico. Santa Anna was training an army of some thirty thousand troops, three hundred miles south of Monterrey. Between lay Saltillo, a large mountain town, and beyond that an impassable desert over which Santa Anna's army would have to march before reaching the American lines. General Wool was at Monclova ninety miles away, holding the northwest flank position of the American army, but it was doubtful how long he could stand an assault from a major attack.

Warren came into the room, clean shaven and neatly brushed. "News for you, dear fellow," he smiled. "Señor Don Luis y Romero has returned to Saltillo with his family. He has a very beautiful daughter and has brought a niece equally as beautiful, so I am told!"

"Who is this Señor Romero?" Blake asked curiously.

"A representative for the Department to the Mexican Congress," Warren replied gaily. "He shipped his family away when we took possession of the city, but learned we're civilized, at least the regulars, and brought them back. They're an old Castilian family and very well cultured. The army knows he is working for peace so he's not bothered."

Blake laughed, "You think a couple of guys like us can crash that sort of society?"

"Why not?" Warren grinned flicking ashes off his cigar. "Thought you'd be interested. I got an invitation to dinner and can bring along a fellow officer. Hear the cousin is a dark-skinned beauty who has something to do with the fight against Santa Anna!"

"What's her name?" Blake asked giving Warren a sharp glance.

Warren grinned, "I don't know, but I thought any woman would look good to you after all these months in the field."

"Not any woman," Blake replied turning to avoid Warren's intense gaze. "Don't get ideas either. There's nothing between Fortune and myself. She seems to be pretty well taken care of by Dennis."

"Sorry," Warren said. "Now get dressed and we'll be on our way."

Pleased with the prospects of dining out Blake moved into the next room to the washbasin and prepared to shave. His mind was surging in curious channels making excitement boil through his lanky frame. The niece might be able to give him information about Sarita. But did he really want to know anything about this girl after what Zaskq had said?

He shaved quickly, bathed in a tub of cold water and put on his uniform. When he returned to the other room Warren was lying on the bunk smoking a cigar and reading some papers. Blake said, "I had a letter from my mother today."

"What's the news on the home front?" Warren asked.

Slipping into his jacket Blake replied. "Same old stuff. That this war is being fought to see who can become the next president, including Senator Thomas H. Benton, of Missouri, who has a son-in-law Captain Fremont, trying to win California for us. Frankly, I've got a bellyful of politics, and neither do I like Taylor because of his attitude toward West Pointers. But I've got to admit he can fight a good war, and that Polk ought to leave him alone."

Warren sat up, and slapped Blake's shoulder playfully. "Come on, old timer," he said. "This outing will do you good. Get the bugs out of your brain!"

A misting rain brushed against their faces in the cold darkness as they stepped from the barracks. Warren picked up a sputtering lantern from the doorstep and walked ahead through the rain to the horses at the hitching rail. Mounting, they rode across the town passing squads of soldiers constantly policing the streets to protect the American troops from attacks by the natives.

The night was cold but soft with a gentle rain beating against them. The creak of the leather and beat of hooves on the street were music to Blake's ear. Leaning back he forgot everything except the prospects of meeting somebody who might know Sarita. He wondered where the Mexican girl might be this night, and if her brother's words were true.

Saltillo was a larger town than Monterrey and built so high in the mountains the climate was quite cold despite its southern latitude. The buildings were made of clay, forming square blocks hardened in the sun. The troops had hardly enough wood for cooking, because most of it was hauled into the city by muleback from the valley.

Bells began to ring. They were rung constantly for meals, between meals, and for special occasions, so it seemed to Blake that bells were ringing at every hour of the day. Each time one rang, the natives, no matter where or what they were doing, would uncover their heads, cross themselves and pray.

They rode up the street, which was dimly lighted by gas lamps and candles, to a large door hanging in an old, moss covered stone wall. The buildings around it loomed like grotesque shapes against the curtain of the cold, rainy night.

Warren signaled for him to halt and pulled a rope by the side of the gate which rang a bell inside the wall. Shortly the ancient countenance of a servant, who appeared to be a part of the stone structure, opened the gate and let them inside.

He took the horses and turned them over to a small boy, then led the Americans up a flight of stone steps into a large house. Inside the officers found themselves in a wide parlor lighted by flickering candles in a huge overhead glass chandelier. The furniture, drapes and carpets showed elegance, wealth and refinement.

Señor Don Luis y Romero, a tall, olive-complexioned widower, with a black mustache and almond eyes, greeted them with extreme politeness like that of an old Spanish nobleman. He introduced his daughter, a tiny girl with large, black eyes and hair, and dressed in a brown and white

93

gown. She had the faint mustaches which were considered marks of beauty among the Castilians. Then Señor Romero sent for his niece.

While waiting they passed pleasantries, speaking in English, which the host and hostess did most fluently. Blake puffed amiably on the cigar presented him, not having enjoyed such luxuries for many years, but wondering why those strange, invisible drums had started in his mind again.

He turned his thoughts to his host in hopes of forgetting the sensation. Señor Romero was a cultured man who lived in style on great landed estates Blake never dreamed was possible. He was of that race which settled Mexico from the cream of the Latin world, the nobleman who came there after the conquest of the country and lived in greater splendor than in Spain.

Blake pulled his ear thoughtfully when disturbed by the rustle of thick skirts, feet moving softly down steps beyond the glass door of the room. Excitement began to race through his veins, for it seemed that every cell bcame alive in his body with anxiety to see the woman who was approaching the room. The drums became a roar in his head.

Suddenly they stopped and he felt the pull of a powerful magnet turning him to find Sarita Gonzales standing in the doorway, her beautiful black eyes fixed upon him. His first reaction was that this was a vision. Something in his imagination, beyond his physical reach, as haunting as lovely music.

"My niece, Señorita Gonzales," Señor Romero's voice broke his spellbound rapture.

She wore a foam white gown of lightweight silk, ruffles which spread in a sweeping richness around her, and supported by the stiff hoops underneath. The neck of her gown was made in a low V shape showing the purity of her golden flesh. Her hair was the color of a raven's wing, a glossy, jet

94

blackness which fell in thick rings around her shoulders and sparkled in the candlelight.

"Lieutenant Blake," she murmured in rich, precise English, curtsying. Her voice was soft, a wonderful contralto like April winds in the pines.

"Ah, Señorita Gonzales," he said bowing. "We meet again."

She smiled mysteriously with a twinkle in her eyes, soft lips curving aginst dark flesh. He suddenly thought of her standing on the high banks of the Rio Grande that day in Matamoros, the lovely vision of the dream impressed in his mind. Yet, he could not forget what Peddar Zaskq had said that night before the campfire when coyotes howled in the darkness.

He stood looking at her with rapt attention and the hush was like a stillness before the storm. Only the servant announcing the dinner broke the spell and taking his arm she led him into a broad, splendid dining room. He hardly knew what he ate, so wrapped was he in the immaculate, breathtaking beauty across the table, for it was really the first time he had an opporutnity to fully see her outside his dreams.

She was the girl at Matamoros, the lovely bronze beauty poised gracefully against the sky. She was the girl clad in boy's clothes escaping from Matamoros; the girl on the battlefield at Monterrey, and the girl which Zaskq had told those terrible things about, that made men duel over her and kill one another. She had been a controversy of dreams.

After dinner they had liqueurs in the great hall again. She turned, her mouth blending into the continued smile, a flutter moved her eyelids and made something tender and secret of her whole face, as if she knew exactly what he was thinking.

"You are wondering about me," she murmured softly pouring the wine from a decanter into a shimmering glass for him. "Yes, I am the friend of your guide, Peddar Zaskq. You desire to know why I am here?"

She paused, then continued. "There is work to be done to save Mexico. I am fortunate to be the leader of our cause for peace, under God's banner. We work for the security and peace of our people. Santa Anna is the tyrant that rules and we must overthrow him in a peaceful manner. Therefore, I also work with you, the American army."

"Why are you here, in this house?" Blake asked curiously, the others were drawn to one side of the room, and he could not be overheard.

She replied in her rich voice. "I am having a series of conferences here with some of our people who have just returned from Santa Anna's camp at San Luis Potosí. They have brought important news. My Uncle who is a member of the Mexican government and in complete sympathy with our cause, is sitting with us. Through him we hope to bring our message before our Congress which is now in session."

The loud clanging of the courtyard bell stopped his reply. Almost instantly the old servant appeared with Sergeant McQuillen who saluted and handed Blake a paper. "Orders, Lieutenant," he said briefly giving the girl a hungry look.

Blake opened the paper to find the division had been ordered to leave for Monterrey within two hours. Turning, he bowed to the girl, and his host and hostess, apologizing for the disturbance, explaining: "The army is withdrawing from Saltillo. I've orders to report to headquarters at once!"

Sarita took a shawl from a hall rack and putting her arm through his walked through the courtyard. As they neared the horses which had been brought around to the steps by the old servant she pulled him into a small archway and thrust a package into his hands.

"Please carry this to my friend," she whispered. "It's my Uncle's reply to Juquila who asked him to spearhead the peace movement in Congress. Guard it with your life and my love!"

He gazed deeply into her luxurious black eyes, in a spell of enchantment, her lips so close, so inviting. He leaned

96

over and put his lips to her mouth. The world spun into a thousand shivers and suddenly blended into one white shining light.

He stepped back and saw the tears in her eyes. She pulled away sharply, hands holding him off. "Goodbye," she whispered. "Perhaps we will meet again someday. Perhaps!"

Whirling he strode to his horse, mounted and without looking back rode off, hating himself for what had happened. To have been taken in by a pagan. Zaskq was right, the woman's beauty was fatal to any man who came near her.

He became aware of the package in his hand and thrust it inside his jacket wondering if she had told the truth, or was it information on the American army, being routed to the enemy? He would be a fool if it wasn't turned over to headquarters; but she had trapped him, and his conscience would make him carry out her command.

He was a fool, a bitter fool!

Chapter Seven

Blake entered the regimental headquarters during the early gray of the morning dawn on February 16, 1847 and saluted Colonel Calloway. "You sent for me, sir?" he asked pleasantly.

Sitting at his desk writing reports the old officer looked up with a dark expression in his brown eyes. His handlebar mustache fairly wiggled with some hidden springs of emotion. "Yes, Blake," he spoke in a voice edgy with an undertone of resentment. "I want to talk with you."

Hauling up in the fading lantern light Blake frowned suddenly from the surprised shock of the Colonel's insinuation. "Are the Indians still after my scalp?" his slow smile held a contempt that was not good natured.

Calloway stroked his mustache studying the young officer. He wondered if it was a mistake in calling Blake and speaking too soon about the growing rumors that kept cropping up on his Chief of Scouts. Matters were rapidly getting out of hand anyway. Scott had instructed the Second Division, under Worth, which included the Eleventh, to prepare for the march to Brazo Santiago, a point at the mouth of the Rio Grande. There the troops would board a transport and join the invasion fleet under Scott for the assault on Vera Cruz.

Polk had ordered General Winfield Scott to succeed Taylor in Mexico to neutralize the latter's growing popularity.

Scott was authorized to carry out plans for an attack on Vera Cruz and possibly a march on the Mexican capital. He arrived at Brazo in late December, and proceeded up the Rio Grande to Camargo to meet Taylor, but the latter was at Victoria, a city south of Saltillo, establishing a military post. Without consulting Taylor the whole field army was stripped for the assault on Vera Cruz, leaving only a few dragoons and two field batteries.

"There is dirty talk about you, Blake," Calloway's voice was unfriendly. "I've heard rumors that it was your family record that got you off the hook on that court-martial. Now don't go off your rocker. Nobody can prove anything!"

Blake took off his fatigue cap and ran a hand wearily through his stiff hair. "Good Lord, Colonel," he swore in a discouraged voice. "Who is it now? Dennis?"

"It could be Dennis," the old officer felt sorry for Blake but he could not let his sympathy get the best of him. "I really don't know, but you've made a fool outa him a couple of times. Not intentionally, but for one thing he seems to think you and Fortune are sweet on each other, and this makes him jealous."

Blake said puzzled, "I do like Fortune. In fact I have thought about asking her to marry me. She hasn't any business running around the army. What she needs is a home, family and security."

"Ain't you being noble, Blake?" the old colonel's lips twisted in a half smile. "Maybe you wouldn't marry Fortune as easy as you think. She's a real stubborn woman and got a mind of her own, just like Mary. But I've got an idea it's that crazy Dennis who is putting a lot of silly stuff in her head about riding with the troops."

Blake asked soberly, "I don't know what to do. I'm really mixed up. I'm tired of all this fighting among ourselves and would like to go home one of these days with a full skin, marry, settle down and live like decent folks."

"You're dreaming, Blake!" the colonel snorted. "It ain't in your blood. You're just an old war-horse like myself, and

100

if your enemies in the army don't get you, the Mexes' bullet might."

"What's this talk about, Colonel?" he scowled with a kind of weariness in his face. He wanted to get on with it and quit playing with words.

"It's funny, very funny," the colonel said flatly with cold courtesy in his voice and his direct gaze warning Blake. "Not so much you as that funny guide, Zaskq. No factual evidence but the finger of guilt points at him."

A faint anger stirred in Blake. "Can we stop talking in riddles, Colonel?"

"Everything comes by word of mouth," Calloway said sharply. "Didn't you attend a dinner party in the home of a Mexican legislator in Saltillo? Wasn't Zaskq's lady friend there and didn't she give you a package for him? You handed him the package and allowed him a three day leave!"

Under the Colonel's unrelenting gaze Blake searched back in memory, now, recalling that only McQuillen or Warren knew what took place that night. Suddenly a thought came to him with such abruptness that he looked at the old officer with searching carefulness. Maybe McQuillen talked out loud and it got back to the headquarters.

"Yes, that is all true. But those people are supposed to be members of a peace party in Mexico!"

The colonel said with undisguised sarcasm, "Confound it, Blake. That ain't your job to get mixed up in this sort of thing. Let them work through headquarters if they want to cooperate with the army. I'll give you a good piece of advice. Just stick to army detail and leave everything else alone!"

"Yes, sir," Blake said stiffly.

"You leave such matters alone in the future," Calloway repeated sharply. "And keep this talk confidential. If Zaskq's doing anything wrong we don't want him to find

101

out that we know, and fly the coop before we put our hands on him. Now get back to your bivouac and pack up for the march to Brazo Santiago. We're due to sail upon arrival there."

Blake hesitated a second then left the tent knowing that it was useless to put up a defense. This was ended and the colonel thought him a fool, he concluded bitterly. Ever since the campaign started there had been a growing chasm between him and Calloway.

The army moved across the plains to Matamoros where the troops were put aboard steamers for the coast. From there the route lay along the beach with waves beating around the ankles of the marching troops.

Blake and his scouts dismounted and led their horses along the water's edge crossing the strait of Boca Chico, which separated the mainland from the outer stretch of land against the sea, on a footbridge, carring their luggage by hand and pulling stubborn horses.

They arrived at Brazos St. Iago at sunset on the fifth day and despite a heavy gale went aboard the transport Huron, via small boats. Four hundred men and twenty officers were crowded aboard the ship along with the horses and pack animals and regimental equipment.

Twelve thousand regulars and volunteers were drawn from Taylor's army and sent to various Gulf and Atlantic ports to assemble at the Lobos Islands, a good port approximately halfway between Brazos St. Iago and Vera Cruz.

General Scott reached the Lobos by ship, from Tampico, on February 21st, where he found the transports loaded with troops from the First and Second Pennsylvania, South Carolina, and parts of the Louisiana, Mississippi and New York regiments of new volunteers.

Within a week many more troops, including all the regulars of the expedition, arrived from Tampico or the Brazos. The natural breakwater that protected the anchorage, a sandy coral island of about one hundred acres fringed with surf, covered with wild orange, lemon and lime trees, hid itself behind the spars and cordage of nearly a hundred ships.

Smallpox broke out on one of the ships and the army was put ashore. While the ships were fumigated and cleansed the men were patiently drilled by the drum, fife and bugle. Meanwhile, the general waited impatiently for more surf boats and heavy ordnance, and the large transports requisitioned in November, while making plans for the assault on Vera Cruz.

"Here comes the rabbit," Warren nodded toward the starboard side of the ship where Lieutenant Douglas was making his way on the rolling deck, toward them. "Wonder what Old Handlebars wants now?"

Blake sitting with Warren on the forward deck of the Huron, practically alone, looked up. "I don't know," he remarked. "Let's wait and see!"

"You know what's a good thing to do with him?" Warren grinned with a devilish light dancing in his dark eyes. "He needs a ducking to take some of that importance out of him. And I'm just the guy to do it!"

"Hey," Blake exclaimed anxiously as Warren rushed off. "Wait a minute!"

He sighed wondering what Warren was up to, and let his eyes briefly gaze at the sea sparkling in the brilliant late sunlight. The spars of the American invasion ships were silhouetted against the lowering sun in a blue sky. The fleet was anchored near a point called Anton Lizardo, just outside the harbor of Vera Cruz, having arrived there several days before.

103

The high peak of Mt. Orizaba appeared in the distant blue sky like burnished silver. The castle of San Juan was distinguishable in the distance, a fortress, protecting the harbor of Vera Cruz. Numerous English and French trading ships were at anchor in the harbor.

Douglas came up wearing a natty, blue uniform. "Where'd Warren run off to?" he barked. "I've got a message for both of you from the colonel!"

Blake studied him. The aide had certainly changed from the day of his arrival at Matamoros, just before the first battle. He had changed from a scared rabbit into a strutting fool, giving everybody the impression that he was the mouthpiece for the colonel.

"What's the message?" Blake asked quietly.

Anger crept into the aide's face, but he swallowed hard. "The colonel says to meet him at the gangplank by four thirty. General Scott has called a staff conference aboard the Massachusetts at five o'clock. You and Warren are to go with him!"

"Yes, sir," Blake grinned.

The little officer threw back his head, turned and marched off across the swaying deck. Blake watched him thinking that Douglas was too young to be given the responsibility of an aide-de-camp to a regimental commander even though he had been through the northern Mexico campaign.

A fresh wind swooped in from the west rocking the ship. The lapping water against the wooden hull made a particular kind of music. Sea gulls circled and mewed around the stern of the ship waiting for the troops to throw their supper remains overboard.

The deck was practically empty of troops who were below getting their meal. Blake watched the little officer proceeding to the starboard side inwardly flinching at what plot George Warren might be hatching up for him.

The aide marched under the side ladder. Just as he passed the signal shack Warren dashed out of the door in such a hurry he apparently didn't see the young officer opposite the gangway. His timing was perfect for he barely brushed Douglas, but enough to throw the aide off balance and send him spinning through the opening of the gangway, his hands frantically clutching for something to hold. A loud dismal wail was cut short by the splash of water.

"Man overboard!" Warren yelled racing for a life buoy. He threw it over the side and disappeared into the nearest passageway.

The Navy watch officer sprang into action and with the help of several sailors had a Jacob's ladder over the side. He climbed down to fish Douglas out of the water and pull him aboard.

The commotion attracted a large number of soldiers who gathered around the top of the ladder and, when the aide climbed aboard, let out gales of laughter. He stood there shriveled, bedraggled and trying to smile, but was filled with too much humiliation. His burning glance roved over the crowd coming to rest on Blake. It lingered there with a warning rage. He turned, stalked over, head high and his eyes brimming with tears.

A high girlish laughter turned Blake. He saw Fortune standing on the upper deck with Dennis. There was dark suspicion in the officer's eyes as he glanced toward Blake. Blake turned away and went into the passageway.

Warren was in the cabin. "You crazy fool," Blake said hotly. "You knocked the kid overboard purposely. This might get you in pretty serious trouble!"

Warren roared. "Nobody can prove a thing. I doubt if anybody saw it. Besides that ought to shrink his swollen head!"

"I admit he had it coming but you didn't have to use such drastic measures!" Blake replied seriously. "The kid's sore at you and will get even someday!"

"What'd he want?" Warren asked stopping his laughter.

"Scott's called a staff conference on the Massachusetts at five. We've got orders from the Colonel to escort him.

We're supposed to meet him at the gangplank in a half hour!"

Warren nodded and chuckled. "That's the funniest thing I've ever done. I don't think I'll ever get over laughing at him going over the side!"

Blake wondered if this meant real trouble for the dark faced Lieutenant. He said. "You've pulled your last practical joke. The time when you put whiskey, instead of water, in the colonel's canteen went undetected because the old man was too busy with headquarters details. But little Napoleon's got pride and will have his revenge!"

Colonel Calloway was waiting alone at the gangplank when Blake and Warren arrived at the appointed time. He regarded them silently as he returned their salute and ordered them into a whaleboat.

They were rowed across the choppy sea by a crew of the Huron's sailors to the war steamer Massachusetts, flagship of the American invasion fleet. A blue flag with a red center waving at her main truck indicated that General Scott was aboard. Blake looked at it wondering what the future might be in this land of strange contrasts, deserts, mountains and deep jungles.

He turned his attention to the colonel hunched over, sitting in the bow of the whaleboat, his countenance filled with a brooding expression. He felt a deep psychic current flowing from the old officer and this disturbed him though there was nothing more than the fact that Calloway did not like horseplay among his officers. Warren had humiliated his regimental aide and something should be done about it. This started Blake to worrying.

They reached the Massachusetts and went aboard. Most of the regimental commanders and their staffs had already arrived and gone to the large smoke filled cabin which served as the conference room. The talk among the officers was a low heavy murmur. Blake and his party took their seats in the back of the cabin.

Simultaneously General Scott stepped into the cabin. The discussions stopped instantly and a deep electrifying current went through the audience. Every officer sat up and watched Scott closely. Blake felt the deep thrill penetrating himself, realizing the electric force from Scott was actually charging the room.

Scott was a tall man, at least six feet four inches, weighing about two hundred pounds, his body as hard and fit as that of a man in his middle forties. His frosty blue eyes were keen and his small mouth drawn up tightly. He was a massive imposing figure, erect, domineering and challenging, dressed in a goldbraided coat and heavy bootstraps with a saber clanking against his thigh.

General Winfield Scott was an extraordinary leader. Blake knew that the United States thought of Scott as the real father of the American army. Scott was a Virginian and had fought in every American war except the Revolution of '76. He was in his prime, a man of sixty, saddle-hardened and the keenest mind for warfare.

He was, however, politically ambitious, a friend of every president and the favorite hero of the nation. Polk knew this ambition and was forewarned of what might happen if Scott stepped into the war at the outbreak of hostilities. The old general would return to Washington with a brilliant war record fresh in the minds of the people and defeat any presidential candidate the Democrats could muster. So at the first sign of war Polk put Taylor in charge of the American army in Mexico and assigned Scott to a desk in Washington.

Scott set his plumed chapeau on a table and looked at his staff officers with stern granite features. Seated around the table was his general staff, referred to as his "Little Cabinet." There were: Colonel J.C. Totten, Chief of Engineers; Lieutenant Colonel Ethan A. Hitchcock, Inspector General;

First Lieutenant Henry K. Scott, Assistant Adjutant General; and Captain Robert E. Lee, Engineer Corps.

Beside them were the Commanders of the Army: Brigadier General William J. Worth, USA; Brigadier General David E. Twiggs, USA; Major General Robert Patterson, (Volunteers); Brigadier General John A. Quitman, USA; Brigadier General Gideon J. Pillow, (Volunteers); Brigadier General James Shields, USA, and their respective staffs.

Scott opened his conference in a serious tone. "Gentlemen, we are on a sad note this evening. Word has been received by headquarters that Santa Anna attacked General Taylor at the pass of Buena Vista, February 22nd, and defeated our army. This is all the detail which I have of that battle. So there is little need to ask questions.

"Now to get down to the business at hand. We will go ashore tomorrow at three a.m., with Worth's division in the lead, to be the first to land. The Eleventh Regiment, under Colonel Calloway, will be thrown forward in advance of the army at dawn, three miles below the city to draw the enemy's attention while the main part of the army gets ashore.

"Order your troops to carry nothing but an overcoat, a haversack with four days' provisions and a canteen of water, besides their arms and ammunition. The dragoons and scouts are to land with the Eleventh. Their mounts will be put ashore as quickly as possible."

The general's voice droned on with the plans while Blake's thoughts turned to the report of the battle at Buena Vista. He wondered if the sick and wounded on the battlefield had been slaughtered by the Mexicans? He knew what this would mean to the troops aboard the ship for, already disturbed over the invasion, they would probably become panic stricken with fresh fears. The news of Taylor's defeat meant that Santa Anna could gain the support of his people and make a supreme, enthusiastic effort to throw back the Americans.

His mind went to the prank aboard ship earlier, and wondered if the colonel's aide would make charges against Warren. Slight anger skidded through him for he was too involved in army problems without having more added to his burden. He turned back to General Scott and listened to the discussion going on between the Commander-in-Chief and the staff on the details of the landing of the troops at Vera Cruz.

The blood in his veins pulsed like drumbeats. He identified this with Sarita and his thoughts began building up a slow excitement. Were these the Drums of ECK?

Chapter Eight

The white summit of Mount Orizaba was boldly etched against the flaming dawn on the morning of March 9, 1847. Fortune Calloway, disguised as a trooper in the dragoons, leaned against the ship's rail watching the feverish activity among the ships in the fleet as the troops prepared for the landing at Vera Cruz.

Filled with excitement she gave her attention to the officers of the Army and Navy shouting orders in clarion tones, above the din of soldiers roaring their favorite airs, and the musicians playing away at the national anthem. Brightly colored signal flags fluttered gaily from the mastheads of the American ships.

Fully half of the army, including the Eleventh Regiment and the dragoons, under Dennis, among whom she had secreted herself, were put aboard the frigates Raritan and Potomac before dawn. Dispatch boats dashed frantically through the swarms of whaleboats collected for the purpose of putting the troops ashore.

Proud of her successful disguise Fortune responded to the action swirling around her which reached its zenith about eleven o'clock, when amid thunderous cheers from the throats of almost ten thousand troops the Massachusetts plunged through the fleet and took its place in the lead. A gentle southeast breeze filled the sails of the war vessels and transports and they were soon in line behind the flagship.

Everywhere her glance roved she saw foreign warships with their yards and riggings black with men. On the decks of the anchored packets in the bay, women stood under fancy parasols gazing curiously at the American war fleet.

By one o'clock the fleet arrived near the Sacrificious Islands just off the coast of the mainland and a few miles below Vera Cruz. The ships dropped anchor and immediately three signal flags arose on the main truck of the Massachusetts. The landing operations for Worth's brigade proceeded at once.

Fortune went over the side of the ship, with the dragoons, knowing that if discovered she would be sent back to the ship. Dennis had ordered her to stay away from his troops but instead his strength and contempt for her had unwittingly impressed and won Fortune. She saw in him the same fire that was in Henry Blake and stayed as close as possible to the officer at all times.

Dressed in buckskins and looking like a slim boy with ugly knives and guns jammed in her belt Fortune descended the side of the ship with the first wave of troops. She carried a small carbine and wore her pigtails tucked under a fatigue cap. Other than the men with her nobody would have recognized the girl, and they gladly kept it a secret as a boost to their morale.

She sat in the rocking surfboat awaiting the operation to commence. The colonel and his staff, including Blake, the scouts and part of the officers of the Eleventh were in the sixth boat to her right, but they were too busy with the landing operation to notice the occupants of the other boats.

Sixty-five boats were finally loaded with at least fifty to eighty soldiers in each, then pulled in a long double line to the quarter of the steamer Princeton. Several hours were consumed in the operation and she was exhausted from the heat on the water. The loading operation was finished by six o'clock.

A strange silence suddenly fell across the waiting army in the surf boats. Excitement started pounding in Fortune's head as she looked up and saw Mount Orizaba standing sharp and clear against the distant horizon, its peak glittering from the setting sun in a deep, blue sky. Not a ripple marred the burnished water while seagulls wheeled above them, mewing and crying.

This was a mystic moment, the pause before the attack when every man was thinking of death, or God. The flash of a signal gun from the Massachusetts boomed across the water breaking the spell. The surf boats cut loose and oars flashed in the setting sun. The late afternoon light glittered on fixed bayonets attached to dull-polished muskets. Regimental colors fluttered at the stern of each surfboat making the excitement of the operation spin her senses.

Cheers burst from the throats of the troops. Music rolled from every ship in the American fleet. The guns of the fortress of Vera Cruz and Ulúa thundered on the evening air, but the distance was too great to be effective against the American landing operation. A Mexican cavalry stationed on the beach to resist the invasion was routed by shells from the Yankee gunboats.

A surfboat sped ahead of the landing operation and went aground on a bar several yards from shore. General Worth, a gallant figure in blues and plumed chapeau, leaped out and waved his saber. He was followed by his officers. The whole brigade was instantly in the ground swell holding aloft their muskets and cartridge boxes.

Fortune waded ashore with the troops as the regimental flags were planted in the soft sandy beach. Companies were formed and ordered to charge the rolling dunes beyond where the enemy was expected to be found, but to their disappointment the foe had fled. Patterson's division followed from the ships and shortly afterwards came Twiggs' regulars. By mid-evening more than ten thousand troops were encamped on the dunes.

Scott landed the next day while the surfboats continued to bring in artillery, ammunition and supplies. During the next few days the lines of American troops were established completely around the city. Long trenches were dug, gun positions constructed, roads leading into the city blocked, and the water supply cut off.

Fortune rode reconnaissance with the dragoons despite anything that Dennis could do, short of reporting her to the colonel. She had secretly and cleverly escaped the restrictions placed on her and got to the battlefield where she was unobserved by the officers who were too busy preparing for the siege of the city.

"You don't have any business riding with the troops," Dennis said in an annoyed voice to Fortune as they sat by the campfire the evening of March 22nd, after General Juan Morales, Mexican commander of Vera Cruz, refused to surrender the city and Scott's siege guns opened their bombardment. "I'll be hauled on the carpet if the colonel finds out."

She turned to him. Her green eyes flashed in the firelight, like windows of a soul looking upon the world with an eagerness to fulfill the loneliness in her life. "I should have been born a man for I can't resist battle," she said. "What's wrong with me? All I ever wanted was Henry Blake, to live with him, please him and raise a family. Now I'm cast into this wilderness with nothing but men, guns and a flock of camp women!"

Dennis gave her a cold, hard look which indicated that he was infuriated at what she was doing, emotionally dedicating herself to a dead man. He should send her away. She was too irresponsible.

He said, "You're committing an error which may ruin my army career by continuing to slip in with my troops and ride in battle. If you are injured I'd be dismissed at once from service!"

"Does it make much difference, Frank?" she asked looking at the leaping flames. A glowing ember fell through the burning wood and died in a smoking blackness. This was like her life blazing in the night, then dying away in a

114

smoky ruin. Out in that wilderness was death for her. She knew it and could feel it.

In this moment Dennis realized that she was gradually coming under his domination and flinched at the thought. He didn't want the responsibility of this wild kid on his hands. He would get the blame regardless of the outcome. He said, "It does make a difference, Fortune. Now get out of my hair or I'll report you to the colonel."

With this he rose quickly and left her sitting by the campfire alone. After awhile she raised her head and listened to the roar of artillery fire against the city of Vera Cruz. She detected the sensitiveness of her position, but why did God put her in this awful position?

Did she have some divine duty to fulfill? Was it the revenge for Henry Blake's death that kept driving her on? The fulfillment of the law of God, an eye for an eye, or a tooth for a tooth? Or was she to have the God-appointed mission to lead the army into the city of Mexico?

A vision swelled into her mind. She saw herself riding at the head of the troops, leading them into that wondrous capital of this dark, mysterious land. An ecstasy of joy surged through her, seemingly bringing relief to the problem which had vexed her so these past weeks.

She rose to her feet listening to the rising crescendo of bombardment. The city walls blazed like a sheet of fire while shot, shell and rockets struck in spurts of red flame. She heard a fierce roar. A shell with an ignited fuse mounted higher, paused, turned and then with swiftness dropped into the city crashing a roof. A terrific explosion followed shaking the earth under her feet, then she heard the screaming, wailing and terrified yelling of women and children.

A cold fear shivered up her spine, like a crawling snake, but her mind was too strongly taken with the emotion to give heed to the warning which was trying to break through to her physical senses.

Sergeant Barney McQuillen let his horse pick its way through the rubble of the streets, in the city of Vera Cruz, followed by a detail of scouts which included Bush, Osborne, Hultkrans, Campbell, Fontana, Arnold and Michaels. The remainder of the scouts were with Blake at the temporary regimental headquarters on the southeast side of the city.

They had been ordered to reconnoiter the captured city to estimate the damage of the American guns and see if there were any cache of arms hidden anywhere. He remembered the violent sounds of increased suffering and consternation that came from the city while the American gunners fired into it. The sound was a pandemonium of confused and frightful noises, bells ringing, terrible explosions, the earth quaking and rumbling, crowds of screaming women and men wandering about the city streets crying for surrender.

This awful, ghastly specter of blood was a joy to McQuillen. His respect and admiration for Scott was growing. The sounds of the beleaguered city had been music to his ears, and his joy overspilled when word reached him that Scott refused to halt the guns when requested by the Spanish, French and British consulates at Vera Cruz. He demanded complete capitulation of the city allowing neither women nor children to leave.

After four days of bombardment, the city walls were breached and plans made for the American assault, when General Landero, new commander of the Mexican defenses, surrendered the city. Terms were quickly agreed upon and on March 29th the garrison marched out, stacked their muskets and surrendered their small arms, then departed into the interior on parole not to serve in the war until duly exchanged. The citizens of Vera Cruz were guaranteed protection of their property and freedom of religion.

"How far are you going, Sarge?" Arnold asked for he was sitting sidewise in the saddle.

116

McQuillen grinned. The red scar on his stubbled cheek gleamed in the warm sunlight. "To the alameda. Thought we might find tequila. The lieutenant wouldn't know the difference."

The domes of Vera Cruz were shining in the bright sunlight while those palms which had not been struck down by cannon fire stirred in the soft southwest breeze. Hundreds of buzzards floated in wide circles far above the stark, blackened ruins.

They reached the alameda and found it in ruins. A Mexican youth came out of the basement of a building whose walls were standing stark against the spring sky. Dressed in a close-fitted, blue jacket, gilt buttons and red sash he picked his way through the rubble unconscious of the scouts who had halted their horses and sat watching him. He crossed the alameda with a jaunty, swaggering stride to a stone house sitting intact among the ruins, where a small street urchin was perched on the steps, and disappeared through a door.

McQuillen raised his gaze and saw a dark, young woman, in a pink dress watching them from behind the curtains of an iron rail balcony on the second floor. A hunger rose in his chest, and he raised his hand motioning for the scouts to follow.

They halted at the house where the urchin sat. "Señores, desean tequila?" he shrilled.

"He wants to know if we'd like a dram of firewater, Sarge." Hultkrans exclaimed. "How about it?"

McQuillen glanced around carefully and saw the scouts, greedy-eyed, watching him. He glanced beyond them at the bright sails of the fishing boats in the bay and the vast, blue, cool gulf beyond. To the left was a forest of American ship spars and masts piercing the misty sky.

"Nothing doing," he replied dismounting and looked at the kid. "But I'd like to take a look inside. Could be a cache of arms in there."

117

A sixth sense buzzed some kind of warning in McQuillen's brain as he stood there looking at that decrepit door wondering if he should obey it. But he shook it off and motioned for the scouts to follow. The kid jumped up, ran past them to the door and swung it open. He put out his hand to beg but McQuillen hit him with the back of his hand, pulled his revolver and stepped inside.

He was in a gloomy room lighted by guttered candles on a half-dozen tables. Behind a rickety bar was an old crowbait Mexican in a dirty apron grinning at them. Several brown jugs sat on the bar as if weighing it down. A boy in a broad sombrero was slouched in a chair with a serape thrown across his shoulders, and strumming a guitar.

McQuillen looked around for the dude who had entered the house but nothing indicated he had been there. He quieted that alarm within himself, and went up to the bar wondering if this could be a trap. A crowd of Mexes could be hidden behind those curtains in the passageway at the back of the room.

The bartender aroused himself. "Tequila, señores?" he asked.

McQuillen's eyes glittered. Reaching forward with his left hand he started to swoop up a jug, but the bartender moved with amazing agility and raked it away. "Dinero?" he grinned.

"Money!" McQuillen growled shoving his gun back into the holster and threw a handful of silver across the bar.

More silver clinked on the surface as the scouts crowded up grabbing jugs, all but Osborne, the squat farm boy from Missouri, who stood to one side watching them with narrowed eyes. A rustle of curtains in the hall had attracted his attention. A flash of skirts and the low whisper of women's voices reached out and made him suck in his breath deeply.

His glance swung back to the scouts again but they were too busy at the bar. He began a slow advance along the wall toward the curtains watching to see if anyone saw him.

"To old Scott!" Arnold said lifting a glass.

"To the colonel!" Campbell replied breaking into a jig. "Hey you with the guitar give us a tune!"

The guitar player's face cracked in a wide smile. He started strumming his instrument. McQuillen's brain began to buzz again with that warning as he walked over to a table and seated himself. He loosened the gun in his holster and sat there studying everything in the room knowing it wouldn't be good to keep the men in there too long.

Suddenly he straightened up. Something was wrong, but he couldn't grasp whatever it might be at the moment. He counted the scouts. "Where's Osborne?" he said abruptly.

The noises in the room stopped. Everybody looked at him. Bush ventured the scout hadn't come in with them. McQuillen sent Bush and Michaels outside but they returned empty-handed. Osborne was forgotten instantly and the gaiety started again.

McQuillen scratched his head, then counted noses again and wondered about the scout as his gaze came to rest on the curtain in the hallway. He stared at it with a question hammering in his brain.

He began to get nervous. The men were off guard and the lieutenant would tear his hide off if he came back without his full squad. He had to find Osborne. He raised his voice. "That's enough! Get outside to your horses!"

Grumbling the scouts started for the door. When they all had left the room McQuillen drew his revolver and treaded lightly toward the curtains. The old Mexican jumped from behind the bar with fear in his face. McQuillen's left fist drove into the wrinkled, monkey-face. The old man went down.

He pushed aside the curtains and stepped into the dimly lighted corridor. A door on his right took his attention. He looked at it fully conscious that his back was a target for a knife. The whimpering of the old man echoed faintly down the passageway.

Softly he turned the knob and kicked open the door. Horror stopped him quickly. The missing scout was lying face down on a wrinkled bed with the flame of a low candle flickering on a knife handle that protruded between his shoulder blades.

His gaze swept around the narrow room and lit upon the dude with the red sash around his waist squatting on the floor with a pretty woman, counting silver coins. Blind rage slowly climbed up his spine into his brain.

Simultaneously they sprang up. The money clinked against the floor as a single dollar rolled around his foot. The woman crawled rapidly over Osborne's body across the bed and huddled against the wall like a trapped animal. The dude pushed up against the wall with both hands flat against it, stiff as a board, his eyes rolling with fear.

A deadly hatred thrust itself into McQuillen's brain. He pushed the revolver into the holster and drew his knife. That awful feeling of lust for killing seeped into him — an uncontrollable passion which ruled him in the time of violence. Stepping close to the cowed youth he grabbed him and slashed the dark throat. As blood spilled on the cobbled floor, like dark wine, a joy swept through him.

Slowly McQuillen turned and stared darkly at the woman huddled fearfully on the bed.

His big hands grabbed her hair brutally snapping back her head. She whimpered, pleading in a rapid Spanish that made little sense to him. With a quick movement he kicked her hard and slammed her against the wall. He stared long at the dead scout rubbing both hands against the sides of his pants.

The scrape of shoes in the hall whirled him to find Burkhart the young bugler, in the doorway, eyes wide with horror. McQuillen was instantly at his throat holding him in a vise-like grip.

He snarled, "Keep your lips shut about this. Else I'll slice your throat wide at any time! Promise?"

120

"Promise!" the bugler gasped.

McQuillen shoved him away and pointed at the dead scout. "We'd better get him out!" His foot struck a silver dollar, and squatting he scooped it up and pocketed it. "You grab the feet, I'll take his arms!"

McQuillen spoke again as they moved along the corridor with their burden. "What you doing here?"

"The looey sent me to find you guys. The army's getting ready to move ag'in."

McQuillen packed the body on a horse and strapped it down with ropes. He turned to the scouts. They were sober, but he knew they were cowardly and would stick together in misery. He said, "Osborne got knifed while lagging behind. I'm going to report it that way. Anybody got objections?"

They nodded silently but their eyes swung toward the bugler.

McQuillen said in a deadly tone. "The kid ain't got no objections. Have you bugler?"

Hultkrans pulled his horse to a stop in the shade of the broad oaks and wiped the sweat off his jaws. He waited for the two scouts, Campbell and Ichler, to come abreast.

They pulled up beside him and drank from their canteens. Upon finishing both turned to Hultkrans as if expecting him to take the initiative in the talk. Ichler leaned across the pommel watching his companion's face closely.

After awhile, Hultkrans said, "You guys remember that night in Monterrey when Riley said the Mexes would pay ten thousand pesos for any native working against Mexico?"

The scouts nodded silently.

"I got a scheme that ought to get us that cash," he said with the light glistening in his eyes.

"What kinda scheme?" Ichler asked.

Hultkrans rolled a cud of tobacco around in his mouth and looked patiently at the distant chain of purple mountains reared up against the horizon. The maguey plants with their clawlike spikes on gray-green fibrous leaves covered the landscape. He turned back to the scouts.

"That so-called American guide of our'n," he said softly studying his companions with squinted eyes. "He's spying for somebody. And I bet he is part Mex under the skin."

The silence was broken by the snorting of the horses. Finally Campbell said, "I don't know. Maybe Zaskq's working for us. We might get in trouble!"

"But who'd know it?" Hultkrans demanded.

Ichler shrilled, "What difference does it make? Reckon the Mexicans would like to pay a few pesos for any of their kind serving with us. They wouldn't know till it was too late they'd brought back their own, eh Hultkrans?"

"How we gonna do it?" Campbell asked picking his teeth with a cactus thorn.

Hultkrans grinned, "I'm gonna contact Riley tonight and see if his offer still stands. Then we'll set out to catch that character."

"Yeah? But how?"

"You know he goes to the pond every night to wash up before bedtime. Riley can post some of his gang around to catch him. I'll collect the dough and split with you. Two thousand pesos each. Nobody'll ever know the difference!"

Campbell growled. "I don't know about that. It don't sound so easy to me. Maybe that traitor won't pay off!"

"I'll tend to the collection," Hultkrans muttered wrapping his fingers around his revolver butt.

Blake left his tent and stepped into the soft darkness. The sky was filled with huge, blazing stars and the night closed around him like a chilly wrap. His scouts were huddled around the bright campfire.

The army would leave Vera Cruz at dawn. Heat, fatigue, bad food and yellow fever would soon strike at the army unless Scott moved immediately into the mountains. The destination was a beautiful little town called Jalapa, seventy-four miles beyond on the road to Mexico City.

He was worried about Fortune riding with the troops for Scott would learn about it and there would be trouble for all concerned. Meanwhile the colonel was held responsible for her conduct while with the army.

The scouts stirred around the fire with what he thought restless movements. They were all there except Zaskq who had gone to a nearby pond for his nightly ablutions.

The new scout, Jim Plummer, who had been assigned to the detail was bragging about his military feats. He was rapidly becoming a nuisance to Blake. Headquarters had assigned Plummer to the scouts from the infantry, over Blake's protest.

He noticed that Hultkrans, Ichler and Campbell were sitting apart from the others, taking no part in the bantering of Plummer. Hultkrans was leaning against a tree staring down at the pond path with dark eyes. McQuillen sat alone, wrapped in a blanket, in a brooding mood.

Blake thought about that knifing episode. He was bound to lose men on patrols but the scouts had backed McQuillen's story. Only the bugler looked pained when questioned yet his answers were like the others, so Blake wrote his report and sent it to headquarters.

Suddenly he got an urge to talk with Zaskq and walked down the path toward the pond. The night closed around him and the trees loomed gloomily on both sides giving him a strange feeling as if he were moving into a black pit. His eyes became accustomed to the darkness and the brush and tree trunks grew into his vision.

All at once the soft beating of the drums were inside Blake's head. It came so swiftly that he stopped in the path.

He remembered that those drums were always inside him when something menaced him. This was a warning, but so strong that his hand dropped to his gun and pulled it, while at the same time he crouched in the brush, aware that something ominous was about to happen. The only sounds, however, were the noises of Zaskq splashing in the pond. He decided it was a false alarm and stood up.

A twig cracked somewhere in the nearby darkness. The alarm went off again in his head. He jumped forward listening sharply. Feet suddenly thumped in rapid succession against the earth and voices in staccato Spanish crackled on the night air. Zaskq's voice shouted in reply.

Blake pumped his legs into action. He broke through the brush with his revolver out ready to fire. Two squat figures in broad sombreros were pushing Zaskq away from the pond with carbines against his back. He was coming up the embankment with his hands raised.

Blake yelled, "Duck!"

The guide flung himself against the earth. A rifle flashed and a musket ball whined by Blake's ear. He fired twice and heard a body thump against the earth. Then he was running toward the thicket pulling at his knife. Somebody came out of the starlit darkness at him. They met with a shocking clash, like giant prehistoric animals in the night, grunting and swearing. Blake went down with the attacker on top but with a sudden switch of his hips rolled sidewise half-throwing the attacker from him. For a brief moment he had the advantage. He drove his knife into the man's ribs.

The man slumped and Blake pushed hard, then jumped up yelling for Zaskq. The thump of hooves against the earth caused him to tear through a brier patch to where a Mexican was trying to force Zaskq on a horse. The captor wheeled firing his short carbine, but Blake was on him fast, digging his knife at the man's breast.

Turning he cut Zaskq's bonds. "What happened?" he asked panting hard.

124

"Some of Colonel's Zapato's men tried to kidnap me," the guide said rubbing his wrists from the rope burns. "They expected to take me to Santa Anna and collect a reward of ten thousand pesos!"

Blake said in surprise. "Why?"

"Santa Anna has put up ten thousand pesos reward on the heads of Juquila, Sarita or myself," he exclaimed in the darkness. "But we must be taken alive. We're dangerous to his ambitions!"

"I wonder how they found out about you being here at the pond?" Blake said curiously staring down at the dead man.

"I'm not certain, captain. But time will reveal that answer!"

Blake suddenly thought of Hultkrans, Ichler and Campbell sitting apart from the scouts tonight. He shook his head doubtfully. It could have been any of the scouts except Williams and the bugler.

"I'm glad you escaped harm," he said abruptly.

The guide took Blake's hand. His dark eyes gleamed like cats' eyes in the darkness. "Lieutenant," he said in a very low voice. "I'm in your debt. You've twice saved my life. There is little need to protest for my life belongs to you until the debt is paid . . ."

He broke off as the scouts plunged through the bush and up to them, guns out.

Chapter Nine

"**H**ello Blake," Warren called dismounting and striding over to the waterhole where Blake as filling his canteen. "How's the spy business these days?"

Blake grinned sourly. "Missed you at Vera Cruz. But that's OK with me. Every time we're together I get into trouble. Been on the carpet twice for something which happened while with you."

"Like that Saltillo dinner?"

"I got dressed down pretty badly by the old man about that. Said I was mingling with the enemy without permission."

Warren squatted and unscrewed the canteen. "Calloway ate my guts out, too. Told me to stop accepting invitations to dine with the Mexicans. But that's tame beside what he did to me for dunking Douglas!"

"I got bawled out for that, too!"

Warren grinned and dipped his canteen into the crystal pool. "Heard about Fortune, eh? She's decided to go on to Mexico City with the army. But Dennis put his foot down and said not with the dragoons. He doesn't want to get himself in trouble with the top command!"

"Fortune's got it in her head that she's going to lead the dragoons in every battle. She and Dennis had a real quarrel about it the other night. He told her to stay away from his command, but she ain't done it yet. There's going to be real trouble, mind you!"

"I hope not," Blake said sadly.

Warren added, "She thinks that she can inspire the troops to victory. And confound it if we don't need some inspiration after that needless slaughter of women and children at Vera Cruz. Every man jack Mexi ought to be priming his musket for us."

The victory at Vera Cruz had turned sour for the army. The useless slaughter of civilians by Scott's refusal to withhold his bombardment of the city, the raging norther which wrecked the transports and storeships, the yellow fever which struck the army hard and the brevet promotions, which ignored the regulars, left the troops on edge. Every man was ready to fight one another on the least available excuse.

The only encouragement received was the official news from Washington that Taylor had not been defeated at Buena Vista as first reported. Instead Santa Anna was soundly beaten and had retreated to Agua Nueva where he reorganized his army and marched south to new positions in a mountain pass known as Cerro Gordo, on the national highway to Mexico City.

Enough mules, wagons and supplies were landed at Vera Cruz to permit Twiggs to march a division of regulars out on April 8th, enroute to Jalapa. Patterson, with two brigades, followed the next day, and behind him came Worth's division of regulars, including the Eleventh Regiment.

The men carried only a pair of saddlebags and a small roll of bedding without tents. The start was delayed until sundown when they moved out over the sandy plains to the north of Vera Cruz, enroute to Jalapa, with Blake's scouts well in advance in a flanker movement to prevent surprise.

The uphill climb for the troops was exceedingly hard on them. They labored all the following day under the burning rays of the tropical sun. Some of the men broke down under the intense heat for they still wore the hot, woolen blue uniform so necessary in their own northern climate, despite Scott's efforts to refit them with lighter garments.

128

Occasionally the army halted at a water hole to refresh and rest the troops.

Blake replied to Warren's declaration about Fortune. "I've had some rumor to the effect that she's with the dragoons but didn't think Scott would allow it."

"She slips away from the colonel and gets into different commands," Warren retorted sourly. "Seems to think that Dennis is the stuff although he treats her shabbily. Oh, say, here comes the colonel now!"

Calloway and his staff rode over the hill and pulled up by the water hole. He dismounted, wiping sweat from his angular mustache, squatted down at the pond nodding to Blake and his companion. He scooped water up in the palms of his hands, and sucked noisily. Douglas followed him, completely ignoring Blake and Warren.

Fortune appeared almost immediately over the knoll riding with Major Dennis and his dragoons. Her honey colored plaits gleamed in the sunlight. Dismounting with an agile motion she stalked across the dead grass to the waterhole where she plunged her face into the water and drank for a moment. Rising she wiped the dripping water off her chin.

"Hello, Jed!" she called across the pond with a mischievous twinkle in her green eyes. "Still in the spy business?"

McQuillen leaning against a tree choked off a guffaw. The colonel stood up quickly, corked his canteen and strode back to his blood mare followed by his staff. Wearing an aura of self-assurance Fortune held her gaze on Blake while a mocking smile curved her lips.

Dennis, lavishly clothed in a red and blue uniform, and a great shako resting in a cocky fashion on his head, came up. He glanced at Blake and back at the girl. "What's up?" he demanded of nobody in particular.

Blake said nothing but stood facing the girl, hands on lean hips and anger pouring through his tough, whip-rod body. The major removed his shako, and wiped the sweat off his brow with his right sleeve. He leaned over to drink.

129

A sudden hostility flowed out of Fortune touching Blake with an impact that shocked his nerves. They glared at one another across the pond with tempers burning in their faces.

She spat words like a fierce tigress. "Why don't you get wise to yourself, Jed? I know more about Henry's death than you think!"

The words numbed his brain. He turned white from the shock. Startled into action by the indirect accusation he jumped halfway across the pond before realizing his action. He landed in the water, splashing Dennis. The girl jerked at one of the big knives in her belt, but Warren grabbed her arms, pulling her around in the opposite direction.

Calloway had one foot in the stirrup but dropped it and turned squarely facing them. His face was a mottled gray. Douglas looked shocked from surprise. Dennis slowly got to his feet with a confused expression on his face.

"What's wrong with you, Blake?" he demanded brushing his jacket. "The heat got you?"

Blake blazed back at him. "No! The heat ain't got me, Major, but your conduct has. You've jeopardized your command by letting that girl ride with your men! You know that!"

Dennis turned purple. He almost choked with rage and humiliation at the accusation. His big fists doubled. "Stop it, Blake." he protested angrily. "How am I going to make her stop riding with my troops when she slips into formation every time we have a fight? I've tried but it don't work with Fortune to tell her not to do anything!"

Blake wheeled and savagely ordered his men to mount up. He leaped into his saddle, twisted his horse around and rode off with Fortune's laughter in his burning ears. He had acted hastily against Dennis.

Fortune Calloway awoke in the late evening, in her tent, with some strange feeling clawing her spine. Her first thoughts were of the incident which happened between Blake and herself earlier that day. For some reason the accusation she hurled in hot words at him had been building up in her mind these past months. They had come to the surface at that awful moment.

The sound of light footsteps outside came to her ears and she sat up quickly. As the steps came to a halt near the curtains she rose and moved to her clothing pulling them on, then took the big revolver out of its holster which hung on a tent peg.

She saw the figure of the sergeant outlined against the tent wall in bold relief from a campfire light. She reached for one of her knives and pushed it into her jacket belt and waited.

The scratching at the curtains revealed he was trying to open them. Sliding across the ground she jerked back the flaps. Surprise completely blanked McQuillen's countenance. His mouth dropped open.

She asked abruptly, "What do you want, Sergeant?"

He moved cautiously coming closer to her, his eyes resentfully studying the gun in her hand. A deep wave of annoyance started working up through her solar plexus into her breast. Her heart beat faster. She knew that look in his eyes, the furtive action of his manner and the feeling that flowed from him. They were the marks of a beast's hunger for its mate. She suddenly knew that she might have to kill him.

She asked him again wondering what excuse he would give for being in her tent at this hour of the night. Yet she was absolutely aware of his reason.

"I've got some news for you, Miss Fortune," he cleared his throat nervously.

"Close the flaps," she motioned lowering her gun.

Moving cautiously he stepped inside and tread lightly to close up the space between them, a heavy, silent figure, alert to the slightest motion on her part. Fire danced in her eyes and her hair was spun gold. The way she stood there with her legs spread, one hand on her hip and chin up defiantly brought a feeling of unrestrained desire in him.

"I've found out something about Henry's death," his whispered breath covered her in a cloud of whiskey fumes. "Want to know about it?"

She suddenly became aware of a deep alarm going off inside her head, and stepped back. It was a warning of danger. McQuillen seemed to be trying to hide his true motives until the proper moment to make advances at her. She tried to shake the idea out of her head.

He took off his hat and scratched his stubbled chin. A smirk crossed his face. "Quite a bit of talk going around camp tonight, Miss Fortune," he continued in a breathless rush. "Nobody likes the way the looey treated you today. The men want to do something about it."

The thoughts went around in her head in an alarming pace. The colonel was extremely angry over her picking a row with Blake and spared no words in telling her. He was alarmed at the significance of the quarrel and the prospects of what it involved for himself. General Scott had told Calloway of his own exacting attitude but came to no decision on the matter.

"What's it about, Sergeant?" she asked.

McQuillen spoke with an unseemly willingness. "I heard from one of the scouts today that it's true. Blake did plan for Henry to take that patrol."

"How did you learn that? Who told you?" she asked without feeling. She was in so much trouble that nothing mattered anymore.

"The kid. I mean the bugler told me. Said he'd overheard it being plotted with that guide," McQuillen muttered.

She trembled with the thought. She had heard from sources that McQuillen didn't get along with the bugler. They had quarreled and the sergeant had given the boy a bad beating. It wasn't logical that he would confide in

132

McQuillen but she was willing to grasp a sliver of truth anywhere, from any source.

The scrape of the sergeant's shoe on the earth startled her. The odor of his thick body flowed out to her senses and she shivered as his hands touched her shoulder gently, comforting her. Unconsciously she leaned against his big chest feeling the magnetism flow from his powerful body. Her gun dropped slowly upon the cot.

She asked hoarsely, "Anything else?"

His eyes glowed like an animal's in the darkness. His breath was hot and smelly near her cheek and a rancid feeling seemed to smother her, clamping the girl in a thick cloud of whiskey, perspiration and unwashed clothing.

He breathed heavily. "I'll get him for you, Miss Fortune. You just say the word!"

Suddenly she came to her senses. Frightened, she pushed at him, jumped back and grabbed at the gun. Missing she pulled the knife from her belt. "Get away, McQuillen!" she cried.

His big hand pinched her shoulder. The odor of her body touched him and twisted around in his brain. It was an animalistic smell, a sort of musk with which the female of the species arouses uncontrollable passion in a man. He pulled at her roughly.

Her heart revolted at this big, ugly beast clutching her. Half swept off her feet, her face scraped by stiff, sandy whiskers as his lips eagerly sought hers, a harsh feel never known before, caused her to jerk at her knife.

Blindly she struck at him. She felt the blade sink into flesh and a joy poured through her. There was a satisfaction about killing something, somebody.

His hands fell away from her. He clutched at his left shoulder. In that brief moment she found the gun and pointed it at his head. The light from a fire outside the tent flickered through the open flaps revealing the deadly intention in her face. McQuillen ripped the knife from his flesh and wheeled, facing her for the kill.

133

"Drop that knife, or I'll shoot you!" her voice hard and low. "Get out of my tent unless you want to die here in the middle of Mexico so the vultures can pick your carcass to pieces!"

He flung the knife down and backed out of the tent into the darkness. Sounds of his feet retreating into the night left her with the desperate knowledge that she had almost killed a man in her own tent. A fact which could have never been explained to a military court. She was lucky, yet it had not solved the mystery of Blake's death.

Blake arrived at the scout's bivouac the evening of April 20, 1847, where he took off his dusty riding gloves and beat them against his thigh. As he reached for the coffee pot which sat on the embers of the campfire, McQuillen, holding his left arm close to his side, passed.

"What's wrong with you?" Blake asked putting the pot on the embers again.

"A Mex stuck me in the fight," McQuillen replied avoiding Blake's eyes. "I'm headed for the medical tent, sir!"

Blake said curiously. "Must have happened last night, Sarge. You weren't holding that arm that way after the battle yesterday."

The sergeant passed on without answering. Blake looked around at the scouts who stared blankly at him from the shadowy darkness. He drank his coffee slowly and turned his thoughts to the battle of Cerro Gordo.

The fight at the mountain pass of Cerro Gordo had opened Sunday morning April 18th when Twiggs' division of regulars and Shields' volunteer brigade marched out before daybreak to climb walls so steep that the men could barely climb them. A previous reconnaissance by Lieutenant P.G.T. Beauregard and Captain Robert E. Lee had opened a way through the rugged terrain so the Mexican's position could be turned. The engineers led the way with the troops following.

The artillery was let down the steep slopes by hand. The men handled the guns, a piece at a time, and drew them up the opposite slope. La Atalaya hill was reached and stormed at two o'clock in the afternoon where Fortune's arrival with the dragoons rallied the troops to drive the Mexicans from the crest. But they suffered severely from a battery on Cerro Gordo peak while pursuing the Mexicans down the other slope.

The column halted for the rest of the day and the following night, when Captain Lee directed an operation bringing up and placing a twenty-four-pounder and two howitzers in a strategic position on the summit of La Atalaya.

At daybreak a picked brigade of Twiggs' regulars, with shells and war rockets screaming over their heads from the battery on the crest, surged down the slope of the hill, up Cerro Gordo and over the Mexican breastworks. The Americans turned the captured guns on the fleeing defenders and the Mexican troops drawn up in the pass below. At the same time Shields' brigade charged the extreme Mexican left. Santa Anna and his cavalry left their guns and fled up the road to Jalapa.

Pillow's brigade, guided by Lieutenant George B. McClellan, of the engineers, charged gallantly against the batteries on the Mexican right, but the volunteers encountered difficult ground and so deadly a fire that they fell back with considerable loss, including General Pillow who was badly wounded.

When the Mexican forces holding the batteries realized that Twiggs had seized the pass in their rear and cut off their retreat a white flag was hoisted. Then Twiggs started up the road in pursuit of the foe with the cavalry and field batteries but Santa Anna was too far ahead for the Americans to ever catch up with him.

Peddar Zaskq's soft lilting voice interrupted Blake's reveries. "Good evening, Captain. Did you see Miss Calloway lead the charge against the Mexican battery?"

Blake nodded and looked at the fruit which the guide was eating. "What's that?" he asked.

"An avocado. It grew wild in Mexico until the early Indians found it to be eatable. Later the Aztecs used it as an important part of their daily meals. It grows so abundantly that the people here don't even take the trouble to cultivate it."

Thoughts gathered swiftly in Blake's fatigued brain like a gale coming up over the horizon. Who was this man Zaskq? Was he, Blake, becoming trapped in some dark intrigue which would disrupt his whole service life?

He asked softly. "Who are you, Zaskq?"

"Your friend," his mouth widened into a smile which seemed to lessen the tension in Blake. "And in debt to you, but that debt will be repaid someday!"

He added, "I'm not really a Mexican as some think, but a native of the states, as I've said before. I serve only the SUGMAD, whose creation here was an ancient race which came out of the sea centuries ago, under the great god Quetzalcoatl and settled in Mexico. Quetzalcoatl, the feathered serpent, is worshiped in our country as the Christ of ancient Mexico."

"You're a strange man, Zaskq," Blake said slowly, more confused than ever. "I've wondered about you!"

"It's because you do not understand," Zaskq scooped the flesh out of the fruit, pausing with it halfway to his mouth. "I'm not disloyal, neither am I a spy as often accused. I've been ordered to your side to serve the United States in the interest of this unfortunate country. My real mission is being an agent of God."

The silence of the night was broken by the sounds of horses moving about, and the distant mating call of a coyote. He did not hear but felt the soft rain falling through the tree boughs. "You've a great love for humanity," he said.

Zaskq looked up with a gentle smile. Confused Blake rose and walked away toward his bedding. He glanced back

136

at the guide squatting by the leaping flames of the campfire scooping out the flesh of the fruit as daintily as if in a drawing room.

His mind whirled fiercely. He couldn't adjust himself to what had happened these past few days. Perhaps it was the bloodshed, the horror of battle and the fatigue in his brain and body. But there was a loneliness in his heart for something strange and beautiful. Then came the far off sound of beating drums, a sound which seemed to grow inside his head. The Drums of ECK.

Blake and his scouts rode at dawn up the national highway toward Jalapa. The highway was littered with the dead of both sides, broken wagons and guns. Frequently marauding bands of Mexican soldiers were seen at a distance, looking like flocks of sheep in their linen or cotton jackets. Occasionally the American artillery rolling toward Jalapa would send a flying shot toward them.

The scouts sang as a group, riding up the battle-strewn highway, mostly to take their minds from the horror of the sights they viewed. Tall, slouching figures, in saddles, their chanting was in deep resonant voices of a forlorn and desolate maiden left behind, and homes where a mother's heart was broken by the absence of her son at war.

Blake was the only one of the scouts who did not sing, his yellow eyes constantly searched the landscape for any hostile action. Along the roadside the Mexican peons, riding their lilliputian burros to market, or working in the fields, stopped and stared awestruck at the scouts.

He realized that despite the overwhelming victory at Cerro Gordo there was confusion among the troops. Many openly cursed their officers, believing the Mexicans were leading them further into the country and would eventually cut the army into pieces.

News arrived telling more of Taylor's magnificent victory at Buena Vista. However, the old general was openly criticized by the president for his tactics, especially in leaving his left flank weak and unduly strengthening his right, which almost lost the battle. Taylor had been saved by the unusual gallantry of Colonel Jefferson Davis' red-shirted Mississippians, and Captain Braxton Bragg's artillery.

Taylor had won four hard fought battles and his officers had not let it fail to be known that he had been deprived of a large part of his army at the very moment when he was ready for battle at Buena Vista. As a result the Whig newspapers proclaimed him their candidate for the presidency.

When Blake spied the enemy they were riding out of the woods, on splendid coal black chargers, clad in brilliant scarlet coats and carrying red and white silken pennants. The sun blazed on the long rows of steel lances. A red, green and white flag, embossed with an eagle clutching a snake in its talons, fluttered gracefully in the wind, as they galloped in a flowing simultaneous motion toward the scouts. A bugle shrilled the sharp charge.

Wheeling in his saddle, Blake yelled at the bugler. "Sound a charge, bugler! McQuillen, order the men out in flank on each side. If the enemy retreats bugle a halt!"

The bugle rang sharply on the cold, mountain breeze. Blake dug spurs into the flanks of his mount. The big, dark horses of northerners, larger, more powerful than the slim, graceful stallions of the southland, quickened into a run, fanning out in a curved line. The scouts raised their muskets as the charge began.

A strange outcry arose from their lips, a long screech ending in a high pitch. It was the yell of the men from Dixieland, adopted by most of the American troops in battle and known as the rebel yell.

They crashed on a mingled roar of yelling, horses neighing and musketry. Blake thrust his rifle into a swarthy face and triggered it as a shiny lance ripped his forearm. Then he was in the open again, having charged completely through the foe's thin ranks. He whirled his roan as a heavy volley of revolver fire from the scouts burst against his eardrums. The enemy was in confusion, a whirling mass of scarlet, flashing steel and thumping hooves.

He yelled at the bugler to call retreat and at a safe distance from the field of action, pulled up and called a muster. All of his men were accounted for and mostly unharmed. He ordered Campbell to report the action to the regimental commander.

Before Campbell had disappeared over a ridge Major Dennis, in his fine shako and trimmed jacket, with Fortune Calloway and a squadron of dragoons, galloped up and halted in a flurry of dust. Dennis returned Blake's salute indifferently and looked around, hot, tired and annoyed at what he witnessed as results of the action. He wiped the sweat off his square chin and gave Blake a hostile glance.

"Got yourself a mess of trouble?" he asked in an irritated voice.

Blake's gaze shifted from the girl to Dennis again. "Yes sir," he said.

"I'll assume command," Dennis said abruptly. "Report to Colonel Calloway."

Blake replied sharply. "My report is on its way, sir."

"Then that is all, Lieutenant," he said. "I'll investigate the field."

Blake flushed at this direct dismissal. "Major," he said hesitatingly. "Are you taking Fortune with you?"

The girl wheeled in her saddle hostility written in her face. Her gaze was fixed upon Blake and stayed there without wavering. Blake gave Dennis a stiff salute and waved his men into a gallop toward the highway wondering what Dennis would find out there in the brush—a Mexican ambush?

They had passed the high ridge and reached the highway when a volley of distant musketry arose from beyond the knolls. Fear squeezed his heart for he realized what had happened. He wheeled his roan signaling for the scouts to follow.

139

At the same moment a dragoon appeared on the hill before them lashing his foam flecked mount. As he came nearer he shouted that they had been ambushed. Blake waved his scouts into action spurring his roan ruthlessly. Just back of the knoll he pulled up to a sliding halt and ordered the scouts to dismount. They rapidly crawled up the slope.

From the top Blake could see the fighting. The Americans were definitely in a trap. Riders milled around in a circle trying to break through a curtain of fire laid down by Mexican infantry in the brush. Fortune was firing both revolvers as her horse galloped swiftly in a circle. Blake shouted for his men to spread out.

The volley of musketry pouring from the scouts' guns surprised the Mexicans who turned their fire upon the knoll. For a few minutes it was a close fight with the foe trying to scramble up the hill in an assault on the scouts while others concentrated their fire on the dragoons.

Blake yelled to fix bayonets but as the Mexicans gained the summit the American cavalry appeared on the horizon, bugles blaring and flags fluttering in the sultry air. They came with blue coated riders spreading across the earth, the sun flashing on uplifted sabers, the Stars and Stripes streaming in the wind.

The skirmish lasted only a few minutes. The Mexicans threw away their arms, ran for their horses and swiftly escaped into the thick woods. The infantry fled in all directions, many of them surrendering by throwing away their muskets and lifting their hands overhead.

Blake watched long enough to see if Fortune was unscathed from the fray and ordered his men to continue their ride toward Jalapa.

He didn't bother to halt to bind his wounded arm although the blood flowed freely, dripping off the tips of his fingers. It wasn't serious and he knew it would soon stop bleeding.

Chapter Ten

The scouts continued their ride toward Jalapa finally reaching Santa Anna's rancho, atop a lofty hill, a few miles beyond Cerro Gordo. Here they halted, rested and bathed in a lovely pool.

They rode up the highway again through the awful scattered remains of the retreat. Dead soldiers rotting in the hot sunlight nauseated Blake. He considered himself battle hardened but the road strewn with the destruction of broken wagons scattered across the landscape disheartened him. Finally they rode out of the chaos, his nerves badly frayed from the ordeal.

They halted within two miles of Jalapa to await the arrival of the army before marching into the city. The highway ran between continuous hedges loaded with blossoms and filled with singing birds. The air was laden with a delicate fragrance.

The army arrived and after dressing rank General Winfield Scott, in full uniform with gold epaulets and braid that gleamed in the brilliant sun, cantered his big, solid white stallion proudly along the lines. He held his plumed chapeau in hand. His granite features, sternly set, broke into a rare smile as thunderous cheers greeted him. He knew most of the troops by name, all the senior and junior officers, and most of the long service enlisted men. It was Scott's army. He had built it into a fighting machine on his own ideas.

The troops entered Jalapa about nine o'clock in the morning with fixed bayonets, colors flying and bands playing. Some of the Mexican girls screamed with laughter at the unkempt appearance and nondescript uniforms of the terrible and victorious Yankees. The crowds lining the streets appeared neither hostile nor afraid. Bells everywhere were ringing out a welcome.

Blake and his scouts settled down on the outskirts of the far side of town near a pond of fresh water beside the highway. Late that evening a dispatch rider from Worth's division going south stopped for coffee and brought them up to date on the latest war news.

Blake half listened for his mind was on Fortune and her escapade during the ambush a few hours before. However, he did hear that near the end of 1846 General W.S. Kearney had marched from New Mexico to California in a southwest campaign. He left behind at Santa Fe a regiment of Missouri volunteers under Colonel Alexander Doliphan who was joined by Colonel Sterling Price with another Missouri regiment, and set out for Chihuahua. They captured the city then proceeded to Saltillo to rendezvous with Wool's troops.

Afterwards Blake turned into his blanket thinking that Dennis was a fool to allow the girl to ride with the dragoons. Sooner or later there would be trouble. He finally drifted off into a troubled sleep.

The colonel strode up and down the narrow space of the regimental tent. "You're going back to the states, Fortune!" he exclaimed roughly. "We've got a whole wagon train of wounded and sick returning to Vera Cruz! You will ride with them. I want you to go and stay with your Aunt Kate at Buffalo!"

Major Dennis had left the tent earlier after ingratiating himself with Calloway by telling of Fortune's place in the battle of Cerro Gordo and the skirmish which took part the day before, and that he had saved her from injury and possibly death. Calloway sick with rage and fear, had sent for her.

Fortune's eyes had turned to a dull, smoldering green flame. She smiled stubbornly. "Long as General Scott hasn't objected, I'll stay with the troops!" she said.

Calloway wheeled and stared sharply at his daughter. The tent was filled with reflected sunlight on the canvas. The sounds of the troops preparing for the march to Puebla flowed in around them.

He realized that she knew Scott, wishing to take advantage of the Mexican panic at Cerro Gordo, was unaware of her escapades, and was hurrying Worth's division after the fleeing enemy troops. It would seem quite agreeable to linger at Jalapa with its little plaza and quaint cathedral, flowers and groves of liquidambar, but Scott wanted to occupy Puebla, the second largest city in Mexico, as quickly as possible.

But the troops wanted to stay here in this paradise of birds, to gaze at the many-hued blossoms of perpetual springtime, feast on glimpses of sparkling beauties playing the guitar in grated windows and giving them occasional glances of fire. The soldiers had learned what campaigning really meant. They had gone unpaid and unprovided for, met with hardships and privations not counted upon at the time of enlistment. Disease, battles, death, fearful toil and frightful marches had become realities.

The colonel swallowed his anger. "There's too much danger for you to be exposed by riding with the troops. The other day's escapade almost turned my hair gray. You must go back to the states."

"Don't try to send me away, Paw," she said firmly.

"We've got enough trouble in the army without you tagging along. Most of the volunteers have seen the elephant

143

and feel that they've won enough glory. They want to return to their families. Out of thirty-seven hundred men we'll have just enough to make one company on reenlistments. The special inducements offered many to remain as teamsters have proven wholly ineffective."

The sunlight streaming through the open tent curtains made patterns of light and shade at her feet. "Then that's all the more reason that I should stay," she replied quickly.

The colonel snorted. "Stuff and nonsense! But are you in love with Dennis?"

She shook her head. "I like Frank and will listen to him, but I'll never love anyone but Henry Blake!" She put her hands over her face. "The closest person I could ever come to loving now would be Jed. He's much like Henry!"

They remained in silence as the army around them hurried to leave. "I don't understand Jed Blake," the colonel said wearily. "Everybody's starting to think he's acting strange. Lots of the men still remember that Florida war tragedy. Some of them think he's turned yellow. Reckon it's just from worrying too much."

"Can't they forget the past?" she asked knowing that her crisis had slid by.

He shook his head doubtfully, "It's not as easy under the circumstances."

"What circumstances, Paw?"

"This is the Florida campaign all over again. We're making the same mistakes. Despite our victories the army's morale is shot to pieces. We're being abandoned by our own troops. The volunteers whose enlistments are up just won't stay. The army is reduced to less than seven thousand troops in the midst of a hostile country where the enemy's forces keep growing. If we retreat the whole countryside will slaughter us to the last man."

She asked suddenly, "Who told you about me riding with the dragoons?"

"Nobody particularly," he artfully dodged the question.

"Who was it?" she pressed him.

"Several people have spoken about it," he said evasively. "But Blake was the one who really squawked about it. And there was Dennis . . . ."

"Blake?" she cried impulsively with anger rushing through her like surging waves. "You wouldn't believe anybody who's a spy?"

"Blake a spy? Impossible!" Calloway snapped. "Don't talk like that Fortune! You're a fool to believe that!"

She knew the mistake was already made but foolish pride kept her hanging stubbornly to the point. "It's pretty hard to swallow, Paw," she said in a hard voice. "But something queer's going on in this army. Remember the incident at Saltillo? And that guide Zaskq was on leave of absence by Blake's permission."

She finished hoarsely. "It's hard to believe that he'd do that to the army and take to the enemy's side because he might have fallen for a Mex woman, or believe we're going to get whipped."

"Zaskq's girlfriend, eh?" he muttered. "What has she got to do with this?"

Jealousy made a hard, painful ball in her stomach. "All I've heard is that she's the head of some secret band working for the Mexican government. Excuse me, Paw, but I've got to run down to the corral and look after my horse!"

A dark, brooding silence hung over the landscape making the night solemn and lonely. The moonlight waned on the silvery crested peak of Orizaba and the night music of the insects increased. Lieutenant Lester Douglas dismounted and turned his horse over to the orderly and walked toward the regimental tent to report the results of his mission to the colonel.

145

The brightness of the lantern lights temporarily blinded him but his vision swiftly returned and he saw the colonel sitting at a box writing in the day book. He saluted. "I've just returned, sir. Are you ready for my report?"

"Yes, Lieutenant," said the colonel laying aside his pen. There was a gauntness about his eyes that made the aide wonder at the awful strain under which his commanding officer labored.

"I joined Blake's scouts as ordered and rode to the city jails to search for any missing Americans overlooked in the first drive to release prisoners held by the Mexicans.

"We were joined by Major Dennis and some of his dragoons while on the way to the city. Only one American was found, sir. An officer by the name of Captain Thomas, of the Pennsylvania Volunteers, under Pillow. He was captured by the Mex the first day of battle and taken to Jalapa on the general retreat. He was more dead than alive but after getting some food and coffee down him he could talk."

Douglas continued. "He said it was the worst defeat the Mexicans had suffered. The peon soldiers ran as fast as they could to get out of range of our cannon fire. Their officers tried to stop them by turning their own guns on the soldiers. It only killed a few. The enemy was so confident of victory that the citizens of Jalapa rode out to Cerro Gordo to witness what they thought would be the rout of the Americans. Fireworks had been prepared along the highway at points to celebrate the flight of our troops. Santa Anna made a public demonstration at the church altar and took an oath to conquer or leave his body on the field. He was one of the first to retreat.

"Captain Thomas said most of the Mexes are for us, and that the common man has his fill of war, and their military caste. They want to be left alone, have their taxes reduced and don't care who rules them as long as they are left in peace.

"The Mexicans had planned to march Thomas through the streets then give him a public hanging. Instead they

146

locked him in a cell and after the battle some local citizens moved him to another jail so their soldiers couldn't shoot him."

The colonel scratched his jowls nervously. "Is it really that bad?" he questioned.

"If the people had guns there would be a general uprising which could be the end of Santa Anna," Douglas replied.

"That's interesting," The colonel remarked noting the eagerness in the young officer's eyes.

"Yes sir," Douglas hesitated then plunged into his story. "Blake and Dennis got into a hot argument over the administration's policy."

The colonel straightened up. "That's a bad one. Who started it?"

"Blake did, sir," Douglas replied. "He made the statement that we ought to make peace with the people instead of Santa Anna. Dennis accused him of wanting to sell out to the Mexicans. Blake got mad and told him that he, personally, was tired of fighting a war for Polk and the president ought to call off the Mexican campaign and try to win the election without the use of murder and rape."

"Dennis said he was yellow and if it hadn't been for Lieutenant Warren and myself they might have fought in the streets."

"Huh," Calloway grunted then dismissed the officer and leaned back in his chair.

He couldn't understand Blake's attitude: a fighting man who was suddenly going in the opposite direction. He was rapidly becoming soft. However, Calloway remembered that many of the regulars were against the war and openly declared themselves so.

The beauty of the landscape caused the tension to slacken in Blake and he turned in his saddle watching the scouts.

147

They were spread over the soft blue mountainside earth in a graceful curved line.

Peddar Zaskq rode beside him giving in detail the report of the morning's reconnaissance including his knowledge of the country about Puebla. The guide was a slender figure without the customary bandoliers, knives and guns most of the scouts wore as their usual attire. Instead he was dressed in his usual manner, blue shirt, and form-fitting trousers. A dark blue cap was pulled low over his eyes, and he rode a giant stallion of a deep bluish color.

There was a twinkle in his eyes. "So I'm accused of being a spy," he spoke in a jovial voice.

"It's no laughing matter," Blake said seriously. "I'm not used to such accusations myself. And they are serious enough to cause a full investigation should the general wish to do so. I've little doubt that he might soon order a board of inquiry to check into the matter!"

Zaskq replied soberly. "There's nothing to be alarmed about, Captain!"

Blake looked around studying the vast expanse of hills, gorges, mountains and valleys studded with white villages. Occasionally the sunlight flashed on a silver cascade of waterfalls half-hidden in the forests. The color of fresh fields of corn and grain were a contrast to the shadows of lazy clouds that receded softly into the deep, blue horizon.

Zaskq spoke again. "What does Miss Calloway say to these charges?"

Blake didn't reply at once. They rode on, with the scouts filing out behind, winding through the clear, cool fragrant woods, every turn revealing new majestic scenes. The ascent grew sharper and the air cooler. Finally Blake said. "I don't know how she feels. I haven't seen her since the cavalry skirmish at Jalapa. But I hear the colonel is deeply worried about her."

"It is her nature to be in a fight; she will never change, even in death," Zaskq smiled.

148

Blake noticed the soft expression in Zaskq's eyes. "You like Fortune?" he asked.

The guide nodded. "But it does me little good, Captain, so the thought is dropped out of my mind. I am a man dedicated to God. Besides I am far too old for her and the two do not mix. Besides I'm pledged to ECKANKAR and there is no release from ITS cause!"

Wheeling he rode off leaving Blake to his thoughts. The officer stared after him briefly then looked around to find that they had reached the Black Pass of La Hoya where for more than a mile they were squeezed between two steep mountains, cleared enough to afford an artillery sweep, and partly fortified, but now abandoned. Seven or eight guns were found and spiked by the scouts.

He rode on at the head of the scouts wondering at his conversation with Zaskq. What did he mean by saying he was far too old? The guide did have an air of being ageless, but couldn't have been more than thirty-five. The thought got into his brain and wove itself into the fiber of his mind as the wind started biting into his flesh. Masses of thick vapor whirling up from the immense gorge suddenly buried the scouts in a chilling twilight.

Some twelve miles further they came out on a sandy plain, set with tufts of coarse grass, and in the distance was their destination for the night, the brown castle of Perote, half hidden under a pine-clad mountain.

Blake found the castle had been evacuated by the Mexicans and set up a bivouac to await the arrival of Worth's division. The castle was a superb example of military architecture, capable of accommodating more than two thousand troops. But the enemy was in such a panic to leave they didn't bother to remove the guns and ammunition.

Worth's division came up about midnight, halting at the castle. Garland's brigade was thrown forward while Duncan's battery took a position some fifteen miles on the left flank to prevent any surprise attack.

They moved again the following morning through a country highly cultivated and brown with wheat and barley. After this the army came out on a sandy, arid plain where steep conical hills of bare limestone shot up from a wide, smooth region.

Shortly before ten o'clock on the morning of May 12, Worth's troops drove off a light attack by Santa Anna's infantry and artillery near the village of Nopalucan. Later he met with the government and municipal officials of Puebla and made arrangements for the American army to enter the city. Later that day, after suffering badly from the dust of the acrid, stony plain, they approached Puebla.

Almost the entire population of the city was there to watch them enter the Mexican town. The streets, sidewalks, windows and balconies were thick with a holiday crowd. The Mexicans showed intense curiosity about the American troops, but were disappointed in the unkempt appearance of the conquerors. Sometimes the Yankees had to work their way through the crowd but finally reached the main plaza without mishap where the men stacked their arms and lay down to sleep.

Blake moved among the scouts looking to their comfort. Surprised he found the bugler's face badly bruised. "What's happened to you Jack?" he asked curiously.

"It's nothing, sir," Burkhart muttered. "Just a little personal trouble, sir!"

"Want to tell me?" Blake asked knowing what the trouble was really about. McQuillen had slugged the boy for being too slow in following out an order. This was a part of the army which the officers were supposed to overlook, or turn their heads away.

The bugler flushed, pulled his lips in a tight line. Blake knew his own thoughts were being telegraphed. A slow anger arose in him. He said again, "What about it, Jack?"

"No, Lieutenant," Burkhart said bitterly. "No complaints!"

150

Blake shrugged his shoulders and walked away. What could be done about McQuillen? It was a normal procedure for a sergeant to beat his men into line, but Blake didn't like this type of discipline. Especially when an officer couldn't hit a sergeant for the same reason.

He looked up and saw that they were near the arcades of the plaza where dolls were for sale in the market stalls and there were row on row of sweetmeats. In the background were the chimneys of many cotton mills. The disturbance quietly slackened in him and he tucked it away in some drawer deep within the recesses of his brain.

The chattering Poblana market girls smiled as he passed. They were slender, little girls with great black eyes, and hair combed over their ears. They wore huge silver earrings, snowy chemisettes partly hidden with a gray scarf, short red aprons fashioned around their waists with silk bands and fringed with yellow, small shoes and large silver buckles.

Their smiles aroused a deep response in him and turning he looked back with fresh enthusiasm but they ducked their heads and giggled fiercely. He went on with new interest and a spring in his stride.

Chapter Eleven

"**S**ounding off about politicians while in the army is really a serious matter," Warren said irritably, walking along the moonlit streets of Puebla. He and Blake were returning to their quarters after a Sunday's exploration of the city.

The moon was a big, mystic, yellow circle in the sky. The cross of the great cathedral, high above the street, was bathed in the golden light. Bells were ringing in low, sweet celestial music. The contrast of peace and beauty with the inharmony which his companion was pouring out brought pain to Blake.

"I only said what I was thinking," Blake repeated stubbornly, wanting to forget the argument. "The only thing we're doing in Mexico is satisfying the politicians in Washington City. Scott took this campaign because he thought it would make him president on the Whig ticket. And Senator Benton is to be commissioned a lieutenant general, commanding the expeditionary forces, the minute Polk wants to replace Scott!"

Warren said sarcastically, "You shouldn't have shot off your mouth to Dennis. It's the second time you've done that. He got sore at your talk in Jalapa when we pulled Thomas out of that Mexican jail!"

"Stop riding me, Warren," Blake said half-angrily his thoughts on the scene in the little Mexican restaurant,

153

a half hour before, when he had quarreled with Dennis and other officers. "I only said what I believed. That's all!"

"What's wrong with you, Blake?" Warren asked. "You don't seem to like the army anymore! You're too much in accord with the soreheads. Is it because the War Department passed over your promotion? You weren't going to get one anyway because of that reprimand!"

Blake shook his head. "For some reason or other I'm just tired of what is proving to be a useless campaign!"

"Maybe you're hiding something, Blake?" Warren questioned in a nasty voice.

Anger in Blake boiled slowly to a high point causing him to stop in the moonlight and survey his fellow officer with narrowed eyes. He knew that they had to separate despite the orders from headquarters that no Americans move about the city after dark, unless in a group of five or more.

"All right, Warren," he said harshly. "We've got to separate before a fight starts!"

"Suits me," Warren retorted hotly walking rapidly away into the darkness.

Blake regretfully watched him. That was what too much drinking did to George Warren. He, then crossed a side street, and went up it making his way back to camp by another route. He was sorry that they had split for if something happened to Warren, he would always blame himself.

He came to a wider portion of the street, and presently found himself in an open plaza before the cathedral, near the point where he had been a few minutes previously. He walked along, pausing now and then to listen for any sound which might mean danger. The full light of the moon bathed the great frowning mass of stone, glistening on some piece of statuary in the towering belfry. The buildings and residences were more like a series of huge stone fortresses than actual homes. Few people were abroad in the dark streets. He moved swiftly through the pencilled shadows hoping to meet with other Americans.

Danger struck without warning. Suddenly there came from behind the crack of running feet. Swiftly, he wheeled drawing his revolver. He saw the dark figures rushing him. They were dressed in black coats and their faces concealed with masks. He met the foremost attacker with gunfire that swept the man off his feet. The second was cracked between the eyes with his gunbarrel, and the third went down with a bullet in his head.

His assailants fell back as suddenly as they came, and disappeared leaving their fallen in the moonlit street. Blake started to slide past the bodies but halted as a woman appeared out of the shadows of the walls. Surprised, he lowered his gun. It was Sarita Gonzales.

She called. "Come quickly! They will be back to avenge their dying friends. I can take you to your army camp in safety!"

She grasped his hand and pulled him along the street hugging the shadows of the wall. She paused under a small archway which ran over the narrow street between the houses and studied the darkness beyond the patch of moonlight on the cobblestones. They listened to the deadly silence, but the only sound was her soft, low breathing.

He looked at her curiously. The girl wore a tight black cap which covered the top of her skull, and a dark tight jacket. As far as he could make out in the darkness her skirt was a flaring ballerina type.

She was graceful, stately, and her oval face, with eyes uplifted at the corners and a large mouth, made him think she was one of those strange people who dealt in the spiritual things of life. The deep thrilling tingle within him was blunted when he thought of what Zaskq had told about her.

He said gratefully, "Peddar Zaskq's debt is paid!"

She laughed, a sound which was like the tinkle of water over stones. "No, señor. He is responsible for his own debts. I cannot pay them for him!"

A stone rattled in the street. Blake looked up to see the skulking figures. Grasping her hand he dashed across the

155

street into a dark alley as gunfire split the night air. They ran for a few minutes, then halted again breathing hard.

"What are you doing here?" he asked panting for breath.

"The same thing. Contacting those who are in the Mexican peace party," she replied. "I was at a meeting tonight and making my way home when I saw you attacked."

She motioned for him to follow. "Come. I've a house nearby where we can go. They will stand around all night watching us. There will be no escape until dawn. Meanwhile, I will send for Señor Zaskq to come and take you back to camp!"

Silently he followed her knowing what it meant for him to be away from camp all night. After waiting for a reasonable length of time George Warren would conclude that something had happened and would notify headquarters. A search would be instigated and if found with the girl he might be accused of spy charges again, or for being AWOL.

Nevertheless he moved along behind the girl through the blackness of the alley. They came to a street entrance, again, paused, looked cautiously up and down the street but saw nothing except the mysterious patterns of dark and gold.

They slipped across the street, went up it a few steps to a doorway which stood in a row of houses, flush with the walk, where she knocked three times. The door was opened by a woman servant. Inside was a small bedroom elegantly furnished. She exchanged a few words in rich, liquid Spanish with the old woman servant, crossed the room and blew out the candle on the table. The room was plunged into darkness.

Somewhere in the house a door opened and closed. "I've sent my servant for Señor Zaskq," she explained. "We'll be safe here until he comes.

"That wasn't necessary," Blake protested uneasily. "I can make it back to camp. The Mexicans will leave after awhile and there will be no trouble in getting away."

156

She laughed lightly. "Ah, señor, but that is not true. I know those scoundrels. They were led by a rascal named Colonel Zapatos, head of the Mexican military police. Nothing would please him more than to capture an American officer, except myself or Señor Zaskq. Each of us would bring him a handsome reward."

"I could get away easily," he argued.

"Not as easy as you think, señor," she said moving to his side by the barred window where he was looking out at the dark street. Nothing was stirring in the shadows. "You see there nothing dangerous, but there is Señor Riley, a deserter from the Americano army. He is in Puebla, as an agent for Santa Anna, just to stir up the citizens against your troops. He will have known by this time about us and sent word to the colonel. But we are safe here!"

"Riley?" Blake ejaculated in surprise.

He turned, conscious of her at his side. The tension ran out of his body like water rushing down a mountainside. The perfume of her hair and body were intoxicating, but he drew back wondering at his thoughts while looking down into her face with deep pools of fire in his eyes. "You've been in my thoughts since that night at Matamoros," he said softly.

She lifted her head smiling. There was magic in the moonlight, a mysticism which had never before touched him. His blood was chilled and his mind became blank.

"I've thought of you, too," she murmured rolling her words softly. She closed her eyes narrowly and peered at him with a strange expression which he could not read. "We can never love until the proper time. The SUGMAD will not allow it."

"I must go!" he said abruptly.

Her hand caught at his arm, wheeling him around. "No, you can't. Stay here until dawn. We will be safe here!"

He laughed, a sound that was hardly more than a deep breath but she heard and stepped back. Off in the distance

157

came the faint, throbbing drums. A tiny rhythm that got into his blood and made his senses spin. He licked his dry lips while studying her with arrogant eyes wondering if she was making this part of a game. If he could determine her motives then it would be good to humble her, crush her proud spirit with one ruthless act. He thought of the tales that Zaskq had told of her fatal beauty to man.

The moonlight burnt into him tearing him into shreds. The desire to humiliate her, to humble her pagan self and make her grovel at his feet was a flame in his head.

He regained his control and stepped back. He thought of his stern Puritan mother, and of Henry lying in the sands under a canopy of stars.

He turned half expecting to find her weeping but saw her standing proudly by the window. He pulled away stiffly.

"We're not even of the same blood," he said savagely making an excuse for that awful guilt feeling within him. Even the darkness was helpful in keeping him from facing her.

Her voice came gently out of the velvet shadows. "You've made a mistake," she whispered. "The glory between man and woman is next to godliness, but your religion compels you to think of love as a great sin!"

He spoke harshly, "What do you know about sin? You're a pagan!"

"I do not know much about your faith," her voice came through the darkness around him. "I only know about life. My God never condemns anyone, but says that love is the only thing in life."

He reached the door and stood by it silently with a feeling, a misery sweeping him. His annoyance that an Indian maid could move him and uplift him was a counter conflict. The orthodox views taught by his mother were a hard shell woven tightly around his mind. His plan of reducing Sarita through humiliation and thus be freed of her had backfired. She had no consciousness of love. She would give herself in the glory of her pagan God.

158

Sick at heart he opened the door and stepped out to find dawn breaking across the eastern sky. Peddar Zaskq arose from the steps where he had been waiting and walked with him silently along the pavement.

Finally he spoke, his tone was the deadliest Blake ever heard. "What is past must be buried, Captain."

"Yes, of course!" Blake said looking at the guide. A cold chill plunged up his spine. "I never wish to see her again."

There was a smoldering flame in the guide's old-wise eyes. "I'm in debt to you and until the payment is made you are safe!"

Blake lay down on the earth, using his saddle for a pillow, at Río Frío where North's division had bivouacked for the night of August 8th, after Scott had taken up the march for Mexico City, the previous day. His mind was on his life, his home and mother, and all the strange things which had happened to him in Mexico. He had a queer sensation of having to put his personal affairs in order because of impending death.

He threw one arm over his eyes to shut out the lowering sun but sleep would not come. The ground was too hard, and his mind too active. His thoughts turned to Sarita. Guilt feelings stirred within him. He had wronged her in hopes of driving a wedge between them but found it reversed the situation. He loved her but the union could never be for she would not give up her pagan belief.

He sat up and pulled on his boots to find the twilight had dimmed and the fires now brightened the night before a thousand tents. The dull roar of voices arose from out of the shadows. The talk was of the dangers the army now faced. Scott had cut the long communication lines that bound him to his base at Vera Cruz. Even the Duke of Wellington who had followed the campaign with interest wrote in the London Times that Scott was lost.

Holding himself to a slow but steady pace Blake moved across the field to the road with uncertainty embracing himself. This was a bizarre picnic, a lunatic house where all were crazy with some unknown terror.

It was as though he was walking through deep water with chilling waves of air trailing him like ribbons. Looking up he saw Fortune riding across the slope on her big bay as easily as though she was a part of the horse. She held her head high, as she came toward him, in a metallic dignity, her lips pale white. The leather jacket was covered with dust and her golden hair caught little glints of the twilight colors.

She rode almost upon Blake before seeing him and quickly pulled the bay to a halt.

He stood spraddled-legged in the road, stuffing his pipe. "You've been riding hard?" He inquired politely studying her face. She was under a deep strain.

The bay danced and snorted. Smiling coldly she pulled it around and faced him. "I've been out with Dennis and his dragoons." Her voice was that high metallic coldness of a woman under severe strain. "Why? What is it? Something wrong?"

Their eyes met and clung coldly in a solid challenging gaze. "I thought the colonel ordered you to stop riding with Dennis," he said.

"He did," she replied shortly.

"We shouldn't be enemies, Fortune," Blake said quietly lighting his pipe and puffing it. "I don't want your hatred. Time's running out fast. We should be thinking about other things."

Her gaze swung away from him. "Are you feeling it too, Jed?"

"Feeling what, Fortune?" he asked sharply taking his pipe from his mouth and suddenly deciding that he didn't want to smoke. He knocked the tobacco out and stuffed the pipe into his pocket.

160

"Death! It's all around us. I doubt if we ever get out of this alive. None of us, including myself. Scott's crazy for cutting the army off from its base at Vera Cruz without supplies. Even Paw says that!" her voice rose to a crescendo of bitterness.

Her words jarred him. The blood pounded like pebbles through his veins and throbbed against his temples and wrists. He stared at the girl with an emotion of passion and amazement. "It's true," he said. "We're all living in the last throes of death."

Her gaze suddenly reminded him of Sarita's eyes that night in Puebla. This was different, the difference between love and hatred. Peddar Zaskq once told him there was only a hairbreadth.

She gave a sudden whimpering cry and slid off the bay into his arms. The perfume of her hair made his heart pound, but his thoughts were with Sarita. She was whispering in his ear. "Oh Jed, I'm afraid. I've never been like this before. Life is coming to an end for us!"

For a brief moment he was lifted out of his body into heavenly ecstasy. "Be quiet, Fortune," he whispered stroking her hair. "Everything will be all right. Scott knows what he's doing. Many of the troops will die, but nothing will happen to you!"

"But I fear for you, Jed," she murmured in his ear, clinging to him. "Henry's gone. You might be next and then my world is lost!"

Surprised he thrust her away staring with a solid gaze. "You don't love me!" he declared. "You love Henry. Even though he's dead, you still love him!"

The fire in her eyes glowed softly. "Yes. I love Henry more than ever, but there are certain things in you which belong to him. My love for that part of you is great. My love for Henry is more than anything on earth and since he is gone it doesn't matter how he died. I don't understand those stories about you. That you deliberately sent Henry on

161

that scouting patrol, that you've spied for the Mexicans and that Lake Royal ambush!"

"A spy?" Blake echoed. "How come you think that?"

"I heard it from different sources. Paw's worried about it, trying to protect you from Scott's ire. You know how little the General likes him. If headquarters didn't need you so badly in the field, Paw says, Scott would call an inquiry and if facts were proven you'd get drummed out of the service."

"Is it Dennis who is telling these lies?" he demanded angrily.

"I'm not sure," she replied. "He hasn't said anything to me about you."

Blake said scornfully. "Why is he so good to you? Want to get you killed?"

"Frank's sore at you about that ambush near Jalapa. Says you weren't needed but rushed in to make him look bad. In spite of the differences with you, he's my good friend, Jed. I'm not in love with him, but he's helped me a lot!"

"Please don't ride in battle again, Fortune," he pleaded. "You might get hurt. Even Dennis has tried to stop you. I'll give him credit for that!"

"I can't help it, Jed," she said tearfully. "When that bugle blows something gets into my blood. I've just got to ride. It's my destiny. If I'm killed it will be while doing something I love!"

"Colonel, you're defending Lieutenant Blake too much!" General Winfield Scott boomed at Colonel Calloway in the army headquarters tent. "What's the reason? Tell me! I want to know!"

Colonel Calloway's confidence oozed away. Scott was always a hard man for him to deal with. His rank of lieutenant colonel was practically frozen after the Lake

Royal fracas. None of the old officers of the line put any faith in him. He glanced at Captain Robert E. Lee sitting to the right of Scott, a tall, dark skinned man with alert eyes and high intelligent forehead, studying the report of the Eleventh's scouts.

The army had marched through the long defiles of the mountains where a hundred Mexican troops could have easily stopped the Americans. The long, blue columns climbed higher through the windy pass near the peak of Ixtacihuatl. On the morning of the third day, they came to the summit of the pass, more than ten thousand feet above the sea level. Below them lay the valley of Mexico in a wisp of shining vapor. Six broad lakes gleamed in the sunlight and brooded in the shadows of the passing clouds.

The valley was cut with ash-colored roads, gleaming canals and straight lanes of trees, studded with walled haciendas, rambling towns and smug villages. Around them were the highly cultivated fields of orange groves and orchards from which peeped steeples and bell towers with roofs of cheerful red tile and gleaming whitewashed cottages.

The army had marched down the winding road from the mountain heights passing along the shores of Lake Chalco, around the southern side of the chain of lakes, then upon an ancient causeway over the isthmus lying between lakes Xochimilco and Texcoco. A rocky hill known as Pen Viejo had been fortified by the Mexicans, and another position at the nearby village of Mexicalcingo heavily reinforced with troops and guns.

Scott halted the army at Atyotla before the Penon fortress, and set about reconnoitering the region. He was at the point of trying to turn Santa Anna's right flank by an attack on Mexicalcingo when a flaw in Blake's report was discovered. He sent for Colonel Calloway.

"Blake went as far as directed," the colonel replied, watching Lee.

163

"My dear Calloway," Scott broke into a rapid speech, his small mouth pulled up tight and his eyes narrowly drilled into the colonel. "You've defended Blake all through this campaign. For what reason?"

When Calloway failed to answer, he continued. "If I'd accepted this report and made that attack it'd cost us hundreds of men, and I'd have to explain the failure to the president. Luckily we found a practical way, a path, around the lake and the hills, across the valley."

Captain Lee interrupted, "My men would have double-checked the enemy's strength, General."

"Right, my dear Captain Lee," Scott boomed. "Right! I can always depend upon your fine judgment. But I've heard too much about Lieutenant Blake's escapades of late. What about that twenty-four hour AWOL, Calloway? Did you do anything about it? What about that guide Zaskq in your scouts? Got rid of him yet? What about your daughter? I hear she's still riding with Dennis' dragoons even after I ordered you to stop her! Explain, Colonel, explain, Sir!"

Calloway drew himself up sternly realizing that Scott had called him in to let off some of the ire which had been stirring inside him. Very patiently he explained his position in the case, but it only served to enrage the old general who shook a long finger in Calloway's face.

"You will kill me with the administration, my dear Calloway!" he bellowed. "My life depends upon your actions, sir! You shall deal out the proper punishment to Blake. Make him an example to the rest of the officers! Let them know they can't violate army regulations!"

Calloway said soberly, "I will correct everything immediately, sir!"

"See that you do, sir! See that you do! And by Jove I don't want to hear anything further about your daughter riding with the troops. That's all, Colonel!" Scott shouted.

Calloway left the headquarters tent in misery. The dressing down which the old general had given him was the worst in all the years he had served under Scott.

164

Blake returned to camp that evening after reconnoitering the region about the hacienda of San Antonio with General Worth, supported by Garland's brigade and a body of dragoons. They had found the place heavily defended, not only in the vicinity of the white castle which formed the headquarters of the hacienda, but for a long distance to the east.

Blake unsaddled his roan and put her into a corral while thinking about the information on the enemy and headed for the campfire where the scouts bivouacked, to find a pot of coffee steaming over the embers. He refreshed himself and then went to the regimental headquarters tent where his report was given to Colonel Calloway.

When he finished Calloway said slowly, "I've just returned from General Scott's headquarters. He's ordered me to administer punishment for your AWOL at Puebla!"

Fatigue and strain suddenly blended in a rage inside Blake. "What's it going to be, Colonel?" he said. He was too tired and irritable to take much.

"Confound it, Blake," Calloway exclaimed annoyed at Blake's attitude. "I'm not to blame. But what would you think it should be?"

Blake swallowed his ire. "As regimental commander you can just about throw the book at me!"

"I've got a good notion to do just that, Blake."

"Why?" Blake asked sharply.

"For one thing you come stomping into the tent with a chip on your shoulder," Calloway growled. "And the trouble you've been in lately has gotten to Scott's ears! He's just finished chewing me out about that report you turned in yesterday. Lee caught a mistake in it. You underestimated the enemy's strength at Mexicalcingo. I didn't like being put on the spot."

"I wasn't sure about that enemy's strength, but was obeying your orders. You directed me to the east of the enemy lines. I could have had a better chance of making stronger estimates by riding both east and northeast."

165

"I explained that to Scott," Calloway said irritably. "But he's not put out about that. It's the Puebla especially!"

Blake said patiently, "I haven't been aware of any misbehavior, Colonel. My explanation about the AWOL is perfectly logical. I had to hole up in the city until daybreak to escape that gang of cutthroats."

"Most likely you were lying somewhere under a bush," Calloway snorted.

Blake went limp, but caught himself in time and straightened up, white-faced and dazed. He wanted to shout at the colonel, but his lips wouldn't open.

The old man raved loudly. "Look here, Blake. I've been a daddy to you! I've done everything possible to save your hide during this campaign. First, you got into trouble about Henry's death, then hit your sergeant, and next started mixing with the enemy. You make it tough on me, boy!"

"Why haven't you thrown me to the wolves?" he asked stiffly.

Calloway's eyes drilled into Blake. "I like you, Blake. Besides I owe you a debt for your Paw saving my hide at Lundy Lane in the war of '12. But you got started out on the wrong foot in the army at Lake Royal in the Florida campaign, and tried to blame it on a mixup in orders!"

A flame of scorching fire burnt Blake's brain. Within a space of ten seconds he relived a lifetime as the truth flashed into his brain. Calloway was at the headquarters during the campaign and handled the orders which came from General Gaines. Reality held him in a tight voice.

"You mixed the orders, Colonel!" he declared hotly, and accusingly with blazing eyes. "You were the cause of that ambush. You didn't tell us that Osceola's Seminoles were swarming all over the swamps. You gave the retreat orders to every command but forgot us in the excitement. I took the blame for the ambush and death of nine scouts. That went on my record!"

Calloway turned deadly pale. He sprung to his feet and stood, his jaw worked swiftly but no words came forth.

"My God, Blake!" he finally yelled in a fearful tone. "You knew after all these years?"

Blake nodded.

Calloway wiped the dripping perspiration from his jaw. "I'm glad to have it come out into the open. It was an awful cross to bear. I've been tormented by guilt; tortured by what you must think of me. Everybody in the command head-quarters knew. That's why I've been a misfit in the army. That's why Scott has always passed over my promotions and never gave me a command equal to my rank. I want to apologize for everything!"

"I don't want your apology, Colonel," Blake said evenly. "But you can make it right by making a public statement of what you've just said in a letter to the War Department and give me a copy."

"No!" Calloway exploded shaking his head fiercely. "Not that! I've only a short time to go in my army career before retiring. I can't risk it. I won't make any such state-ment!"

Blake winced; his mouth sagged open. He started to pro-test but the entrance of Lieutenant Douglas interrupted. Instead he saluted and left the tent exhausted and dazed.

Chapter Twelve

"**B**lake is like the rest of the West Pointers," McQuillen growled while peering anxiously at the stormy sky hopeful that the downpour would let up before the army started its movement across the Pedregal, a jagged field of five miles of murderous lava beds, to reach the next road north, and bypass the heavily fortified fortress at the Penon.

"What'd you mean, Sarge?" Hultkrans asked popping a wad of tobacco into his mouth and rolling it around with his tongue.

"Not many got raw courage," McQuillen replied in a low tone glancing at the scouts huddled around a hissing fire.

"I go along with you on that, Sarge. Ain't many that can stand up to gunfire like an enlisted man!"

The American army had reached the village of San Augustín on August 16th, and halted, for the highway passed respectively the fortified haciendas of San Antonio and Churubusco. Both were strongly protected by large forces of Mexican troops. Scott saw that a direct advance over the open road northward from San Augustín to San Antonio would be too costly in lives.

Two alternatives lay before him: a turning movement through the swampy fields eastward, but the engineers advised against this for the ground was too soft for passage of the artillery; or to go west through the great field of lava called the Pedregal, a molded sea of stone waves which

169

could cut the feet of the troops and horses into ribbons.

After Duncan's discovery of a mule path across the Pedregal Scott decided this was the way and ordered Captain Lee to put the engineers to work widening the path to permit the artillery to move across to the little village of Contreas.

"What are you whispering about?" Williams asked coming out of the darkness to the sputtering campfire where McQuillen and Hultkrans were stuffing their saddlebags with provisions.

McQuillen looked up with a sweep of his pale, domineering eyes and spat on the ground. "Nothing special," he said.

Williams said, "The lieutenant's waiting at the edge of the lava bed for the scouts. Zaskq is going to take us through."

"Huh!" Hultkrans snorted. "I'll bet that we get lost and drowned in a crevice before the night's over!"

"Get a move on," McQuillen said gruffly. "And get the rest of the scouts going!"

Somewhat later in the evening the scouts moved into the rainy darkness, met Blake and joined the troops to move across the slippery bed of lava rocks, over volcanic upheavals and large fissures barely narrow enough for the troops to leap across.

McQuillen was in a foul mood and with the rain soaking through his clothes life had become a torture. He cursed steadily, under his breath, all the way across the lava beds, sometimes literally beating the men to get them over the slippery rocks. When they reached firm ground he found Fortune Calloway hiding among the dragoons, in the front lines of the army, which was preparing for a charge at sunrise on the Mexican position at Contreas.

Daybreak came bright and clear, after the storm, and McQuillen stood in line with the scouts, bayonets fixed, his eyes resting on Blake's back. The scouts had been put in with Company A, and Blake given charge. They awaited the order for the storming of the enemy's fortifications.

170

The Eleventh Regiment had been moved up with three brigades, through the wet ravines leading to the left and rear of the Mexican lines. Quietly, the troops were ordered to reload and prime their rain-soaked muskets and fix bayonets. McQuillen's eyes narrowed. Would this be the hour for his ambition—to see the death of Blake? The thought sent sensations of pleasure through his thick body.

His glance swept sidewise in a long gaze to see a small squadron of red-coated dragoons, with Dennis in the lead, and the blonde girl half-hidden among them. She was pale but her head lifted high looking straight into the fog which partly covered the Mexicans' position. He wondered if Dennis knew the girl was with his troops.

Brigadier General Persifer F. Smith, a slight, round-shouldered man with blue eyes, sandy mustache and hair, walked slowly by the troops, inspecting them. A deep tingling thrill clawed up McQuillen's spine for he realized the charge was ready.

The general paused, took out his watch and glanced at it, then raised his head. His gaze swept the front line of troops, like a blue flame, coming to rest upon McQuillen. "Six o'clock men," he said cheerfully as if speaking directly to the sergeant. "Are you ready?"

A low murmur rolled through the ranks. The deep excitement made a pleasant pain in McQuillen's stomach. This was a challenge, for the Americans were to storm the enemy's fortifications with only 4,200 troops. Behind the Mexicans' breastworks was an unknown number of enemy soldiers who might easily slaughter the little Yankee band. Besides, the Americans had only a single round of ammunition.

Smith's gaze darted again along the lines. "Forward men!" he ordered in a quiet voice. His command flowed through the ranks like a quiet, ominous current. The troops moved in unison, a sprawling animal, gaining momentum in a forward rush toward the blinding fog that hid the enemy's breastworks.

171

A furious gale of flaming lead and steel crashed into the blue lines. Sudden death among the troops caused havoc and the Americans paused in their charge, but the officers beat them back into the fight with the backs of naked sabers. The dragoons broke but Dennis rallied them again. Fortune's scream for the troops to hurry was a shrill falsetto above the storm of battle. Her slight figure stood out among the troops as she waved a regimental flag picked up from a fallen color bearer.

A round of grapeshot and musket fire swept the field taking toll of the American infantry that swept upon the enemy's fortifications. A deadly hail of firepower struck the dragoons in a splattering sound. Dennis' charger reared screaming in pain and fear. The scarlet and blue figure was flung from the saddle under the impact of cannon shot.

McQuillen saw the girl leap from her saddle but lost her in the fury of the battle. There was a confusion of infantry brawling, horses neighing fearfully, artillery thundering, mules braying horribly, and women and laborers in a mob rushing to escape. Some of the gunners chained to their artillery pieces died under the storming of the Americans.

The Mexican camp was almost immediately overrun, and the attack slowed to a stop. General Smith walked through the blackened ruins of the fortifications, and stopped near the center of the camp. He glanced at the mopping up operations and drew out his watch. "It took just seventeen minutes," he said quietly to those around him.

The sergeant remembered Fortune was somewhere on the battlefield with Dennis' body. He retraced his steps across the craggy ground to where she was sitting with the deceased officer's head in her lap. He stood looking down into her tearstained face thinking that death was a companion to him, but killing by cannon fire was foreign.

"Let me carry him, Miss Fortune," he said reaching down to take the body out of her arms. "We will take him to the general. His body will be buried on the battlefield!"

Silently, she yielded up the body. McQuillen led the way from the bloody battlefield with the girl following. Shortly, they met Blake who took the body. He left them wondering why the dead man couldn't have been the lieutenant.

Blake had received orders from Colonel Calloway to take full command of Company A and B, and rendezvous with the Eleventh Regiment, at the stone bridge, where together they would join the Second Brigade, under Worth, for an attack to turn the flank of the Mexican army at San Antonio.

He laid the major's body in the shade of a tree and bade the girl to stay there until some of the medical corps arrived. He left to gather up the troops of both companies which had been scattered during the battle. He found McQuillen and, together, they succeeded in mustering the men and marching to the bridge where he reported to the staff command. Calloway told him since both company commanders had been killed in battle that he was to maintain command until the action had been concluded.

They marched for two hours under the hot sun over rocks and through fields. All the while the scouts complained bitterly about being forced into the infantry, and cursed the foot soldiers who laughed, jeered and guyed them unmercifully. Blake silently agreed with the scouts but there was little he could do for Scott had ordered that every available fighting man who wasn't in the hospital be put in the lines for the attack.

The brigade moved parallel to the Mexican lines, moving in flank by heavy columns in a swift march. They were kept just beyond the range of the enemy's cannon fire until nearly twelve noon when the Eleventh, which was at the head of the column, was ordered to pierce the enemy's line.

As the battle extended over a large area Blake could see very little of it, and being busily engaged with the maneuvers of his own battalion had no time for exploring other areas of action. The Mexicans soon broke and retreated and the order for a double march was given by bugle. Soon the whole battalion advanced on the run after the retreating foe. They stumbled wearily across the rocks and lava beds to the highway and followed in hot pursuit.

The road proved to be a broad causeway with cornfields and pastures on each side, divided by wide ditches filled with tall corn water from three to six feet deep. Blake ran swiftly, followed by his scouts, and the troops of both companies stringing out behind, with their muskets held in front of them. He was amazed not to have seen any wounded or dead Americans, but the roadway and ditches were littered with the Mexican dead.

It soon became obvious that the Mexican retreat was a trap. They were drawing back to a fortified position which constituted the second line of defense at the hacienda of Churubusco. Blake halted his men and sent word of his position, by his bugler, to the staff command.

Presently Burkhart returned with orders for Blake to advance a half mile and turn left into an open field to join the battalion in an assault on the right flank of the Mexicans' line.

Grumbling, impatient to get into battle, the troops turned into a field and joined Magruder's battery which had formed lines in an open pasture behind a patch of thick corn. The enemy's guns were firing escopeta balls which whistled over their heads and occasionally sang through the corn patch raking deep ruts in the earth.

The American troops, however, stood quietly awaiting orders. Shortly afterwards the battalion arrived and the enemy guns opened with a terrific barrage sweeping the pasture until disorder reigned. The battle got into action before the staff command could issue orders for the assault and continued fiercely on both sides for more than an hour before some order could be established among the American troops. The heavy barrage of the Mexican artillery was

174

beyond anything Blake had yet experienced in his military career.

He shuddered for the din was clashing, the roar of cannons and musketry, screams of the wounded, the awful cry of terrified mules and horses and the yelling of fiercely, fighting combatants all pressed into his brain, in a fiendish, hellish sound.

His battalion had not yet fired a gun, but was moving rapidly into battle, every man eager to start a hand-to-hand combat with the Mexicans. They knew that they could easily outfight the enemy. Colonel Calloway and his staff, including Warren, rode past toward the battlefront.

Warren pulled out and dismounted. "The colonel says I can join the fight with you. I'm ordered to take over Company B. Douglas urged the old man to let me do this with the idea I might get it this time."

Blake nodded. He was glad to have Warren with him. They joined the ranks, and the army moved up, a long, blue line with their fixed bayonets gleaming in the hot sunlight. Blake did not have a sword, so he drew his revolver. Every step he took seemed to produce greater life in his limbs. Glancing around he saw McQuillen with his great, shaggy head thrown back laughing as he marched into battle. The sight made a cold chill work its way up Blake's spine.

He walked on, in lead of the troops, unaware of what was in front of them, whether the enemy was in regular fortifications, behind breastworks, or firing from a cover afforded by hedges and ditches that bordered the highway and fields, and hidden by the tall corn patches.

The battalion came out of the cornfield into a crossroads near some small houses where it was exposed, at once, to a sharp crossfire. The battalion broke and scattered as many of the troops fell under a rain of musketry. Blake rallied the men again and charged the enemy's position, but they broke and fled once more under a fierce round of grapeshot and musket fire which swept across the field taking a heavy toll

175

of the infantry. McQuillen wavered and fell back with the scouts to the rear of Company A.

Furious with anger, Blake grabbed a saber off the ground and tried to beat the troops back into formation. He had one company, whose officer had been killed, to stand, when Major Farrell, of Headquarters Command, arrived and ordered him to make the charge. Bawling orders at the troops he reorganized the three other companies whose officers had disappeared. The troops were made to stand and ordered into the charge with Blake leading when an awful cry arose from the left that the forward troops were being driven back.

The panic turned the men in the front area, and they stampeded through Blake's companies like wild cattle. He yelled at McQuillen to help get order again but the big sergeant tried to join the panic-stricken rush. Blake hit him across the back with the flat of the saber. McQuillen spun around ready to attack Blake but Blake struck him again on the head.

"Get those troops back into line," he yelled hoarsely. "Or we'll all be killed!"

At this moment Warren came up and helped straighten out the tangle of troops. By the time they had halted the panic Colonel Calloway and his staff galloped into the field to take charge of the confused situation. He quickly disentangled the troops, composed mostly of the Sixth, Eighth and Eleventh Infantries and got them in line again.

Calloway ordered the charge from his saddle, his right hand holding a gleaming sword that pointed toward the belching enemy guns. His other hand was in tight reined control of the blood-red mare that danced with fear and excitement.

The wild falsetto yell of the southerners in the lines shrilled above the roaring of cannon fire. The blue line moved forward in a fast run stepping over the bodies of their fallen comrades, naked bayonets gleaming in the hot sunlight.

Every detail of the charge across the scorched earth up to the mouths of the foe's flaming guns was clearly impressed in Blake's mind as he led the troops into the jaws of death. He was like a spectator watching his own body race to the killing. The other self saw his foot step in a dead man's face and slip upon the bloody grass, heard the musket balls whining past his ears, and felt the deep impression of that psychic moment when he stood briefly, alone, on the enemy's breastworks waving the troops into battle.

The surge carried the Americans over the breastworks like a wave of the ocean striking a rocky beach. The enemy gave way, retreating the best they could toward the city of Mexico, pursued by the whole American army, hundreds dying in their retreat.

The dragoons reformed and Fortune rode with them in a charge up to the gates of the city, where the Americans were stopped by a thunderous fire from a Mexican battery covering the entrance gate. Captains Philip Kearny and McReynolds were severely wounded in the fight.

The charge finally lost its momentum and ground to a halt. Blake dropped in his tracks on the field, to sit and drink from his canteen, wondering what had happened to him in that charge across the battlefield into the enemy's lines. He had become a changed man.

After awhile he had satisfied his thirst and poured the rest of the water over his head. Then he went back in search of his scouts and to reform Company A. McQuillen had disappeared so he put Arnold in charge of the company and began to collect the dead and dying. After this he made a search for Dennis' body.

The field was an awful spectacle with the dead thickly covering the earth and swarms of blowflies everywhere. Mangled bodies of artillery horses and mules actually blocked the roads and filled the ditches. Blake searched the field and found several dead and wounded from Company A. He learned that Warren had received a shoulder wound and had been sent to the hospital.

Many of the American dead were so torn by shot that it was impossible to move their bodies. They were buried on the spot without rites, honors or prayers. He finally found the major's body and sick at heart helped bury it, wondering where Fortune might be and how she would take Dennis' death.

Before he finished his gruesome duty thick clouds gathered around the jagged peaks, rolling across the sky. Lightning flashed in great frightful streaks, occasionally near his party. Thunder cracked across the sky and made the earth tremble. He barely reached camp when torrents of rain flooded from the heavens.

Sarita Gonzales rode across the battlefield, with the hot, glaring sunlight reflecting from her white, silken attire. The carnage brought silent grief to her heart and her eyes were filled with a flame of sympathy for those who had fallen in the fury of battle. Her glance swept over the field in search for her American friend who was to meet her there.

Her dark head was covered with a white, brimmed hat to protect her face from the torrid sun. She wore white deerskin gloves and a jacket and riding skirt of the same hue. Her riding boots were made of hand-tooled leather.

Reining her horse on the edge of the battlefield she watched a Yankee burial party in the distance burying their dead. Nearby were the families of those Mexican battle victims searching among the bodies for their own. She waited thinking that it was the will of SUGMAD that had brought this holocaust upon her people.

Peddar Zaskq soon appeared and rode across the battlefield toward her. He was dressed, as usual, in his blue attire. As he drew near she spoke in a soft lilting voice. "I greet you my friend in the name of the Ancient One!"

"God is good to us." The slim man smiled. "Come let us move away from here. There is evil in the air!"

They rode silently down a lane into a deep wood where birds sang sweetly from low, swinging branches. Finally they came to a beautiful stream of swift flowing water and halted their mounts. Dismounting Zaskq helped the woman from her saddle and led the horses across an arched bridge. They reached an upheaval of giant boulders where she dropped upon the grass by the singing waters.

"The American army is moving to Tacubaya where General Scott is establishing his headquarters," Zaskq said as he seated himself beside her. "He will stay there during his truce with Santa Anna."

The girl smiled sadly. "A truce with Santa Anna means very little. But what does he want with the Yankees? Time to reform his army?"

"An armistice which will exclude the Americans from the capital," Zaskq replied. "Neither general can terminate such a truce except by giving forty-eight hours' notice. This enables Santa Anna to build his fortifications for another American attack. He thinks if the Americans can be tricked into giving him three million dollars for peace terms he can pay his men to fight!"

The girl was thinking of Blake and the night at Puebla. Love for the Yankee officer swelled her heart. A tiny squirrel peered curiously from behind a tree, then cautiously crept toward her outstretched hand. It nibbled at her fingers trying to find something to eat, and finding nothing jumped back to the safety of the tree trunk again.

"I am returning to Juquila tomorrow," she said. "I must report failure of the mission. The Holy One will not be pleased."

He replied, "But you're not to blame. He will understand."

"Strange isn't it? The position of the American army. It is a conquering army on a hill overlooking the enemy's capital which is at its mercy, but not permitted to enter, and compelled to submit to all manner of insults from Santa Anna and his followers."

After awhile he said, "Many will die before the city is taken. But you can tell Juquila that Santa Anna is fortifying the castle of Chapultepec and will make his last stand there sacrificing the blood of his own people and the Yanks to satisfy his great pride."

The squirrel peered around the edge of the tree with black, beady eyes. She watched it thinking there was life as given to the world by the great SUGMAD. Life did not seek any particular form, only the soul did. Someday the soul of this little creature would seek a higher form, perhaps the human form.

"You have not failed," Peddar Zaskq said again. "It is I who have failed. I will take the burden for you. I will meet you tomorrow at the Alameda Inn and take you to Juquila and explain what happened. He will understand!"

"Yes, he will," she stood up quickly. "But how little you understand a woman's heart. I am in love with Señor Blake. My love is pure. Do you understand that my brother?"

"Nevertheless," Zaskq replied thinking of the past. "I think you should go through the purification rituals at Chizza."

She laughed easily and ran a slender finger teasingly along his cheek. "You will never understand. Promise no harm comes to the Americano."

Peddar Zaskq smiled. "I can promise you nothing but safety to the monastery."

Only the sighing of the wind in the overhead branches broke the long silence between them. She stepped closer putting both hands on his shoulders. "I love this Americano," she said softly. "I would marry him if he would take me as I am."

He shook his head. "Let Rebazar Tarzs decide what to do. I will meet you tomorrow at high noon in the Inn. Until then I bid you farewell!"

She mounted and rode off toward the city of Mexico, tall and straight like a queen, going deeper into the forest, but her mind upon the white warrior from the north. She kept asking herself if he would come back into her life again and prayed to God that this wish be fulfilled.

She spurred the horse into a faster gallop and turned a long bend in the road, then suddenly plunged into the midst of a half-dozen, dark, sinister faced men. She recovered swiftly and pulled her rearing horse that seesawed against her small but firm grip. Instantly she recognized the coarse, cruel face of the officer who seized her reins. He was Teniente Lazaro, second in command to Colonel Zapatos, of the Mexican military police.

"You're under arrest, Señorita Gonzales," he said.

"I will not resist you, Teniente," she said quietly knowing that her fate would possibly be death.

She fell in between the riders thinking that this might be the punishment for her disobedience to Juquila's request that she keep away from the white warrior from the north. But she loved him dearly and the impossible was only for the gods.

When Blake returned from a reconnaissance that evening there was a message from Colonel Calloway to report at once to regimental headquarters. The old officer was sitting on a cracker box in the twilight, outside the tent, dictating a letter to his aide.

Saluting, Blake drew off his heavy riding gloves and awaited the colonel's attention. Finally the old officer stopped, dismissed his aide and turned to Blake. There was a drawn expression about Calloway's eyes that Blake did not like. He had a feeling it meant trouble.

181

The colonel's voice was tired and weary. "Blake, there's something personal which I've got to talk with you about. I hate to do it, but in the interest of the army it's best."

Blake slapped his gloves nervously against his thigh. "Now what seems to be the trouble, Colonel?"

Slowly the colonel got to his feet, a tall, lanky figure towering over Blake. His face was pale from the surging emotions in himself, and his eyes glistened brightly from behind narrowed lids. He spoke with the heavy patience of a man fighting to control himself. "I ask you as a friend," he said stiffly. "There've been reports drifting in about you having dealings with the enemy. Is there any truth in them?"

"No," Blake said sharply. "What's the foundation of such reports?"

The older man cleared his throat before speaking. "It's about the fight at Churubusco. We lost over 1,056 men, which is more than a tenth of the total strength of the army, due to the fact that the Mexicans knew our general orders far in advance of the time Scott issued them to the regimental commands. We could have threatened the rear of the town and allowed their garrison time to retreat and taken the town, as we took San Antonio without losing a man."

"What's that got to do with me?" Blake asked.

"Somebody gave Scott the wrong information about Churubusco. He was told that it wasn't strongly fortified and didn't have the sort of defense that was put up by the Mexicans." The old man paused fixing his brooding eyes upon Blake. "He claims the report came from the Eleventh. And you're the one who did the reconnaissance of the defense at Churubusco."

"I deny the charge, sir," Blake said in cold fury. "It's preposterous to think I turned in that report. What's wrong with Scott's own spies? He's got Dominguez, a Mexican robber, in charge of his spy company. Maybe Dominguez sold him out."

The colonel said sharply. "That's enough, Blake!"

182

Blake controlled himself. The implications of this war were becoming too much for him. Yesterday he had witnessed the hanging of Sergeant Thomas Riley and other American deserters who were captured at Churubusco where they had manned the Mexican guns. Some of the deserters were branded on both cheeks with the letter "D", then drummed out of camp. They would not get very far in the country where a white man would be killed for the very clothes on his back.

The colonel hawked and spat. "I'm sorry, Blake, but there's nothing I can do if Scott takes action on this. You didn't turn in a written report on that reconnaissance. You know my orders about reports."

"Yes sir."

"Now there's the case of your guide, Zaskq! You've been seeing his Mexican girlfriend? You were with her in Puebla?"

Blake said slowly, "I don't deny seeing Señorita Gonzales, but she's not a spy. I've heard these charges so often, but do you think I'm crazy enough to do anything like that?" He explained briefly his meeting with Sarita that night in Puebla.

The colonel shook his grizzled head. "I don't know what to think, Blake. Dennis is gone. Warren in the hospital in bad shape. Most of my staff killed or injured. This campaign is killing off the best men in the army, and I can't see anything but defeat and death."

He spat again. "Even though we're whipping Santa Anna's army in every battle he's outsmarting us. He figures that we'll run out of food, ammunition and men shortly, just like Cortez did, and then he's got us."

"Now, Colonel, I'm not guilty of all those charges," Blake pleaded.

"I don't think so either, but there's too many reports coming in about you and that renegade guide. You'll have to get rid of him fast if you want to save your neck!"

183

Blake's short, cropped hair bristled. "He's my friend, Colonel." Blake said determinedly. "I can't get rid of him." "That's an order, Blake." Calloway snapped. "Get rid of him right away. I can't protect you any longer!"

Breaking off abruptly the colonel wheeled into the regimental tent. Blake stood there for a few minutes with awful feelings surging through him. There was nothing to do but to tell Zaskq.

He arrived at the scout's bivouac to find Zaskq saddling his mount. The guide listened to Blake's explanation, then said, "It is all right, señor. I am preparing to leave anyway."

"What's this?" Blake ejaculated in surprise.

Peddar's eyes were cold blue diamonds drilling into his face. "Señorita Gonzales decided to return to Juquila to explain why she has failed her mission. Partly, because she had fallen in love with you.

"It is my duty to go with her to protect her from harm that could occur during the journey. I owe my life to you, twice, you know. But I will return to repay you, Captain Blake!"

Chapter Thirteen

Blake led the burial party across the battlefield, his mind and body fatigued from the shock of the holocaust at Molino del Rey. Scott had blundered badly in ordering the attack but shifted the blame to Worth, who was said to have cost the Americans this bloody loss for his assault on the Casa Mata, the Mexican fortifications, without sufficient artillery bombardment.

When the mistakes of Scott and Worth became known the American troops lost faith. both officers blamed the other openly, and the discord between them reached down to the lowest private. Nobody in the American army could find satisfaction in the victory gained with such great cost and difficulty.

Blake missed both Peddar Zaskq and Warren. The latter was still in the hospital and the loss of blood and dysentery left him in such a weakened condition that his life was hanging by a shred. Blake even missed the arrogant Dennis, and yet back of these thoughts his memory was still with the Mexican girl.

He stood by an open grave in the torrid sunlight and filled his pipe, his mind filled with desperate thoughts. He watched the scouts go about their cheerless duty knowing they hated it as much as he. Sooner or later they would break under the strain, go insane under the impact of this horrible task of killing, and become carrion on the battlefield for those vultures floating gracefully through the sky above.

The battle of Molino del Rey was a useless fight and a Pyrrhic victory. Scott had ordered the attack against the Mexican position for the purpose of destroying a foundry which was supposedly supplying the enemy army with munitions and artillery pieces. To his surprise he found himself faced with the whole Mexican army and his attack turned into a full-blown battle which was won after a bloody struggle. He learned that Santa Anna had tricked him for the foundry contained only a single cannon, a few old disused cannon molds, and a small powder magazine.

After the powder magazine was blown up and the captured cannon removed the Americans halted and looked over their ghastly losses. Meanwhile the surviving Mexicans fled up the hill to the castle of Chapultepec which had been fortified for the next attack.

Blake glanced up at the birds of death swinging low over the battlefield. The drums came into his mind, with a deeper and louder beating than ever. He was thinking that now life and death walked together, hand in hand, like lovers. There seemed to be little difference between the two elements of God—life and death. Suddenly he picked up a stone and heaved it savagely at the birds knowing it was a futile gesture.

He thought of the battle again. The information Scott deemed thoroughly reliable led him to believe the guns needed for the defense of the city were under construction at Molino del Rey. He sent a small party under Worth to destroy the works but they found the whole Mexican army entrenched there.

The Americans were driven back several times and their wounded butchered by the Mexicans which only served to infuriate them. Their losses caused many officers to believe that another fight like that would destroy their army. In the Eleventh Regiment alone, the loss was well above forty percent, killed or wounded, Santa Anna's spies had secured a copy of Scott's battle order within a few hours after it was written, and to complicate an already complicated situation, Scott, too, obtained through his spies a complete copy of what was supposed to be the disposition of the Mexican forces before they were entrenched at Molino del Rey.

Blake threw down his shovel and walked away from the detail sick at his stomach, and his mind revolting at the thoughts in it. The charges against him and the impressions of those around him left Blake without any defense for his actions. The disposition of the American army was at the mercy of the country. Uppermost in his thoughts were the continued impressions of death stalking him, like a hunter after a deer. He could not shake the thoughts out of his head.

He unscrewed his canteen top and took a long swig of water, then leaned against a tree trunk. He pulled steadily at his earlobe wondering why he had to live through this bloody holocaust. Why hadn't he died before this?

Footsteps running up the path turned him to find Fortune Calloway hurrying through the woods. "Jed!" she cried flinging herself into his arms. "He's dead! I saw him die!"

"Who's dead?" he asked.

She lifted her swollen face. "George Warren!" she whispered. "He died an hour ago. The minié ball he got at Churubusco was deeper than the surgeons thought. They tried to operate this morning to take it out but he was too weak!"

She sobbed. "He kept holding to my hand calling for his mother. Oh, Jed. I can't take much more of this killing!"

The impact of her words struck him. He held her while staring into her tearstained face. George Warren dead? Impossible! They had been so close. Classmates at West Point, the Florida campaign and Indian fighting in the northwest. It was like having his right arm taken off.

"Let's go back to camp," he said gently taking her arm to lead the girl up the path. "I'll find Mrs. Riley. She will take care of you. Meanwhile, I'll go over to the hospital to see what I can do about taking care of his effects!"

"I've been so foolish, Jed," she murmured dabbing at her eyes with a handkerchief. "Maybe it's best that I go home!"

He wondered silently. How was it possible for her to leave when the Mexicans had cut off the army communications with Vera Cruz? They had to go on to victory or defeat.

McQuillen entered the sutler's tent for another bottle of whiskey. He was still smoldering from the harsh tongue-lashing Blake had given him the previous evening when he was caught striking the bugler.

He went outside and stood in the early morning sunlight sipping at the bottle and thinking about his humiliation. Blake had eaten him out in front of the scouts. Something like that could ruin his army career. He should have talked back to the Lieutenant.

Tossing away the empty bottle he walked across the camp grounds still steady on his feet, and his brain cold sober on plans for Blake. When he arrived at the scout's bivouac he asked for the lieutenant.

"He's out on patrol," Hultkrans told him. "Oughta be back in an hour."

He walked off, his mind cold with revenge. He laid down in the shade of a tree and tried to sleep but his thoughts strayed back to the incident with Blake. Blake had relieved him of duty yesterday morning pending a decision whether charges would be placed against him; just the reverse of what had happened months before. Arnold had taken over the scouts temporarily.

His thoughts drifted beyond his own troubles. Now the fight at Molino del Rey was finished Scott could turn his full attention to the reconnaissance of the city and to the development of a planned attack. The question to be decided was whether Chapultepec might be bypassed for an assault on the fortifications of the city's south side.

The Mexican troops at Chapultepec were not fully armed but they could likely defeat the Americans. The flower of the Yankee army had been wounded, killed or ordered to the rear because their enlistment was over.

McQuillen still believed he had a chance for an officer's commission, and with Blake out of the way might be able to be friendly with Fortune Calloway. He grinned at the thought. He liked spunky women, but first Blake must go, and now was the time.

After awhile the scouts returned and McQuillen sent for Arnold. The corporal came over and squatted down beside him. McQuillen sat up rubbing his head to clear his brain. "Sit down, Whiskers," he ordered.

He picked up a stick and started drawing a map in the dust showing the battle position between the opposing armies. "You got the scouts now," he said. "And you'd better take care of them. See them lines in the dust?"

The corporal nodded.

McQuillen continued. "Now you'd better look at this territory this afternoon, down the field, past the big ridge and over into enemy territory. I think you'll find a couple of high places where you can see the Mex's position more clearly."

"That's pretty dangerous territory," Arnold replied. "It's behind enemy lines. It's possible though for we ain't going to be no more than a patrol of three in that area!"

"Why's that?"

"Don't know except the looey wants only hisself, me and Williams to ride the direction you jist pointed out. The rest of the scouts will go east to explore the Mex's left flank."

McQuillen stroked his chin. "Jist trying to be helpful, Arnold. That's all!"

After Arnold left he arose from the ground, went over to the stack of muskets. He picked out his own, carefully cleaned and loaded it, then hid the gun in the nearby brush. Then he went to Blake's tent and asked permission of the lieutenant to visit the medical tent. Blake gave him a cold, silent nod.

McQuillen came back later and reported to Blake that the medical corpsmen wanted him to stick close to camp for he was developing dysentery. He went back to his blanket and slept an hour, and upon awakening saw the scouts saddle their mounts to ride out of camp.

After they disappeared over the hill in a cloud of dust he arose, saddled up, then got his rifle from the brush. His gaze dreamily swept across the fields toward the high ridge of Chapultepec while his hands gently fondled the gun. He shook off the mood and mounted his horse realizing that his plan was working on schedule.

He guided his horse through a section of camp where he was least known, across a field and along the base of the high ridge, riding slowly but keeping carefully out of sight of the distant patrol of scouts.

Soon he reaced the Mexican lines and worked his way cautiously through it and tied his horse to a tree fully aware of his precarious position.

Blake adjusted his tunic with a quick, angry tug. He was annoyed at Fortune Calloway who had joined the patrol at the edge of camp and refused to leave. Finally he gave in to her whim and signalled for Williams and Arnold to follow. He rode on with the girl at his side, her long, golden tresses braided in long strings, hanging over her shoulders like an Indian squaw.

He was wondering why she had slipped away from the women's quarters just to ride this particular patrol. There

190

were other patrols which could have been far easier to ride. He knew, however, that General Scott had laid down specific orders after Cerro Gordo for her not to ride with the dragoons, but she had disobeyed him at Churubusco where Dennis had been killed. She was confined to the women's quarters since there was no way of sending her back to Vera Cruz as the army's communications lines were cut by Mexican guerillas. He was worried that somebody might report this and he would be blamed by both Calloway and Scott.

They rode north along the Calzada de San Cosme road which was the ancient causeway on which Cortez retreated from Mexico City pursued by thousands of angry Aztec Indians. The city was in no sense a fortified place as was Monterrey, for there were no walls around it, and the gates were only nets of cannons and rifle squads.

The chief strength of the defenders lay in the fact that the gates could only be approached by the perfectly straight causeways that ran through the broad marshy fields flanked by deep ditches. If the Americans used the causeways there would be a holocaust of death with very little cost to the Mexican army.

Blake wondered what Fortune's attitude might be now for she seemed to have recovered from the death of both Dennis and Warren. She was a moody person, capable of giving strong love one day, and fierce hatred the next. But under the circumstances he felt it best to concentrate on the scouting duty rather than be drawn off into quarreling thoughts about her.

Secretly, he was pleased to have her with him. But it wasn't the proper place for a woman. He dismissed his thoughts and directed attention to those points of military interest along the ridge of Chapultepec, making mental notes which would be of importance to Scott for planning an attack on the castle.

Fortune leaned across the pommel of her saddle, her green eyes bent upon him. "Jed," she said in a soft feminine voice. "Are you pleased that I slipped off to ride with you?"

He glanced at her. Fortune was a handsome girl but the six gun strapped to her waist and the dangerous knives thrust through her belt gave her an appearance of a real trooper.

"I'm not!" he replied shortly trying to avoid the subject and keep his mind on the job.

She said gently, "I want to be with you and near you to share your dangers. You are like Henry."

"Henry was a better man than I," he said watching Arnold and Williams spreading out in a flank movement to move forward, several hundred yards beyond. "He had more courage than I. I've come to dislike war. Sounds strange for a Blake to say that. But the horror and killing in this campaign has been enough to last several lifetimes."

Smiling she moved closer to put a hand on his arm. The touch sent a shock through him, tightening his already wound-up nerves, but he wished she would not do this. It was dangerous and he had to keep his faculties alert.

"Jed," she said meaningly. "Forgive me for everything which has happened between us. There is nothing now that I won't do for you. I will marry you if that is what you want."

He reined up suddenly. "Marry me? Why Fortune, you don't love me. It's Henry that you are thinking about. It wouldn't be fair to you."

"It's you that I want, Jed." Her eyes blazed green like jade in the sunlight. "I never knew until the other day that it was you!"

He thought of Sarita and the great gulf between them. She was something that was little more than a dream. Fortune needed him badly and after the war, if they got out alive, they could go back to the states and settle down and raise a family.

He said, "It's dangerous to talk like that now. We've got to be on the alert every minute. Wait until we're back at camp then I'll call on you in proper fashion and ask for your hand in marriage. Right now let's attend to scouting."

192

Her eyes suddenly glowed with a green, magic fire and a beautiful light came into her face. She reached out a hand to him. As he turned a tiny buzzing sound similar to that of a bee whistled past his ear.

The girl's mouth jerked open. A thud in her flesh swung her in the saddle. The big bay leaped and broke into a swift loping run with the girl half over its side.

Blake dug spurs into the roan's flanks racing after her with an alarm going off inside him like a fire bell. When he caught the bay she was lying across the pommel with both hands clutching her shirt. Her blood dripped slowly to the ground sparkling like rich, red wine in the sunlight. Leaping off Blake took her from the saddle and laid the girl gently upon the earth. He saw the scouts coming up fast and shouted for them to climb the ridge and find the sniper.

They returned later, empty-handed, to find Blake sitting on the ground beside Fortune's lifeless body, holding her head in his lap, and stroking her hair. Her wide green eyes stared vacantly at the blue sky and the blood from her buckskin smeared his hands.

Blake made a personal inspection of the Mexicans' position on the morning of September 11th, and sat in conference in Scott's headquarters, although he was dazed and heartbroken over the girl's death.

Among those present for the conference were Generals Pillow, Quitman, Twiggs, Pierce, Cadwalader and Colonel Calloway as well as a number of staff officers. Worth had been excused to make a search for points to establish batteries in case an attack on Chapultepec was undertaken.

The conference turned out to be an argument on whether a frontal assault should be attempted on the castle, or the San Antonio gates. The engineers along with Quitman, Pillow and Captain Lee favored the latter, but Scott concluded the meeting gruffly overriding all arguments by ordering the assault on Chapultepec and returned to Tacubaya to make preparations.

Williams rode in from patrol about four o'clock the following morning, and found Blake still awake in his tent. He made his report, took off his hat and drank deeply from a water jug that Blake offered.

"You'd better say a prayer for all of us, Captain," the Texan declared fervently. "This is going to be the biggest fight we've ever had. The Mex have got more men out there in front of us than I've ever seen in my whole life."

Blake asked, "How many?"

"About fifty thousand, I reckon. We can whip 'em all right, but suppose they run the wrong way. It'd be like a cattle stampede for they'd crush our army with sheer weight and numbers!"

Blake shook his head. "This is the end of the trail for most of us anyway."

The silence that followed was broken only by the tramping of sentries and the pawing of horses in nearby corrals. Insects chirped in the night and somewhere coyotes howled and fought in the darkness. A wind was blowing through the patch of nearby cedars and the low murmuring of furry branches were like voices arguing in some deadly intrigue against the sleeping army.

"You're pretty low, Lieutenant," William, said sympathetically. "I can't blame you, either, after what happened to Miss Fortune."

Blake said with feeling. "I believe that Fortune was the victim of a shot intended for me. I just got a hunch and nobody can tell me differently."

Williams' gray eyes bore into Blake. "I got a feeling about that, too, but I can't prove a thing. I'd swear it was McQuillen we saw scooting out of a thicket. He's been eating his heart out over her death!"

Blake stared grimly at the lantern. "If I find out that he's the murderer he won't last five minutes."

194

"I doubt if you can prove anything, Lieutenant."

"There's nothing more to live for, Williams. I don't have anybody at home except my mother, and she's over seventy."

"I understand, Lieutenant," Williams replied.

Blake pushed the jug aside and sat down on the box. "Give me the news," he said.

"Seems that Scott plans to feign attack with Twiggs' division on the San Antonio gates, by a prolonged cannonade of the palace and assaults by Quitman's and Pillow's divisions with the Eleventh in support. Two batteries have been constructed on the road leading from Tacubaya past Chapultepec, the Cosme road and more on the road from Tacubaya to Molino del Rey. Quitman's brigade was ordered to march at daylight to join Pillow at Piedad where more of our roops are assembled. That's all I know," Williams said. "That's what was picked up around camp today!"

After the scout had left the tent Blake sat in the darkness of the early morning thinking hard. Sounds of the army arousing itself from sleep flowed around him. He extinguished the faint lantern light and lay down thinking of death. His thoughts finally whirled to a stop and he drifted off to sleep.

Sarita sat in a plain wooden chair with her wrists bound tightly by rawhide ropes. She had been held captive by Colonel Zapatos and the military police for over a week. Nothing had happened during this time but she expected the worst at any moment.

A flickering candle threw a soft, low light across the rumpled bed, and the high walls of the room. She had not suffered from hunger for an old Indian servant had brought her meals regularly. The wrinkled, ancient female could not tell her anything for she was a stupid old dolt with little intelligence of her own.

Sarita could not determine where whe was being held, but was certain that her brother was searching everywhere for her. A week had passed since she was to have met him at the inn, and by now he had probably been in touch with Juquila and the search started. The Indians had ways of learning things whereas others could not.

She constantly tried to turn her memories away from the gringo officer but failed. She could not forget that night they declared their love for one another.

Her thoughts were broken by the old servant pushing into the room. "They are here, my beautiful señorita," she crackled.

Lieutenant Lazaro shoved through the door. He grabbed Sarita by the arm pulling her up from the chair. "Come along," he said roughly. "The colonel wants you."

Her heart beat wildly as she stumbled down the dim corridor. They came to a well lighted room where sat the sandy bearded colonel at a table, toying with a whiplash. He stared at her with unblinking eyes while his free hand deftly fashioned a cigarette.

He punched the cigarette into his thin mouth, lit it from a candlestick and sat back with a long stream of blue smoke pouring from his nostrils. "Ah, señorita," he saifd softly. "Do you know why you're here?"

She gave him a faint smile. "Of course I am aware of what you want with me. But I demand that you take me to Santa Anna."

"Let's not joke about this, señorita," he laughed.

"I do not joke, Colonel," she replied pointedly.

He coughed, "Santa Anna is not a fool. He knows that you and your friends have cooperated with the enemy since they have been in our country. Who are the others in the spy ring?"

"There is no spy ring," she sighed.

He leaned closer. "If you'll lead me to Juquila's hideout I'll see that you are properly rewarded. You can be wealthy beyond human desire. You can become the leader of your people."

She shrugged indifferently.

"Santa Maria!" he swore suddenly half-rising from the chair. "You can't hide Juquila. I'll find him anyway."

"You'll never find him!" she smiled faintly.

Her calm enraged him to such an extent that Zapatos cursed her savagely. His right hand shot out like a talon and slapped her hard.

She faced them proudly, completely a queen in her feminine glory, with the candlelight glowing softly upon her golden countenance, a red streak across her right cheek.

"Where is he?" Zapatos demanded hoarsely. "Tell me or I'll lash you with this snake whip, and throw your body to the vultures for their feast!"

Her head lifted boldly with jet black eyes smoldering in the candlelight. "I will not betray him!" she whispered.

He seized the whip from the table and struck. The pain was like searing fire but she did not flinch. Instead she raised her head in prayer and began singing a hymn of praise to her God. The deadly lash hummed its awful melody across her lovely body until a merciful blackness overcame her senses.

She sank to the floor like a shattered vase, her mind drifting down a long pit where the face of Blake the americano officer moved steadily across her inner vision.

Colonel Calloway strapped on his revolvers and drew the leather gloves over his hands then slapped on his campaign hat and left the tent. The American batteries where thundering heavily against the castle of Chapultepec and the Mexican lines near the San Antonio gates.

He stood in the warm sunshine letting his glance travel over the snow-capped mountains, and the green valley of Mexico splashed with red and white blossoms. The sleepy Indian villages and haciendas blended with the beauty of the landscape. Peace seemed to lay over this little world, but he knew that behind the calm was the sinister tumult of war and death.

He was thinking about the death of his daughter and the wrong he had done Blake, but at this moment Lieutenant Douglas' arrival broke his chain of thought. "General Pillow requests your presence at once, sir," he said, saluting.

As he walked toward the headquarters Calloway remembered the final disposition made for the American infantry assault upon Chapultepec. Two hundred and fifty men, including Blake's scouts, and a company of regulars from Worth's division, were ordered to report to Pillow to form a storming party on the castle. A similar party was taken from Twiggs' division for Quitman, and had received scaling ladders, pickaxes and crowbars.

Near eight o'clock Calloway marched with Pillow's party, in lead of the troops, across the open fields, into the swamps where the gray voltigeurs, who proceeded them, were cleaning the Mexicans out of their entrenchments. His feet clumped heavily against the earth and his breath came fast from the pace of the march.

They marched into the shadows of the long, green moss dangling from the giant cypresses with Pillow leading his troops. His leonine head was thrown back, dark eyes flashing as though victory would belong to him, personally, without sharing it with others. Here and there along the advancing line a soldier fell wounded or dead, but the others stepped over and marched on toward the castle.

Everything was a confusing din to Calloway, the yelling of the Americans, the flashing of guns and the crash of limbs overhead, hit by cannonballs, as the forward troops wallowed through the mire and drove the Mexican skirmishers before them.

198

Their advance was made in three detachments. The first consisted of one battalion of the voltigeurs, the Tenth U.S. Infantry, and a small storming party under Blake's command, which moved forward on the outside of the south park wall.

The second detachment moved directly from Molino del Rey through the grounds of Chapultepec while the two infantry regiments under Colonel Troutsdale, and a section of Magruder's battery under Lieutenant Thomas J. Jackson, were sent along the north wall to intercept reinforcements from that side.

The breastworks were captured and then coming into full view of the fort the Americans were met by a sheet of flaming death. The parapets were hidden in smoke and the air filled with the hissing, shrieking and roaring of missiles. Colonel Ransom died, and his troops wild for revenge charged, but only a few reached the moat around the castle wall where they died or retreated under the withering fire.

Calloway grabbed a sword and furiously beat the troops into the charge, but it was futile. The ladders had been thrown away by the bearers who fled from the storm of the battle. The charge died away and the voltigeurs dropped behind the shelter of rocks and stumps, and began firing at the parapet, while the Ninth and Fifteenth regiments deployed to the left and found refuge for themselves. The storming party under Pillow climbed the slippery hill only a short way further, halted and took shelter behind rocks.

Calloway sat with his back against a boulder while sweat poured off his leathery jaw. He offered his canteen to his aide and watched the spasmodic firing of the troops. The ardor of the fighting was cooling as time passed and the ladders had not yet appeared. The American batteries stopped firing and those little mounds which looked like graves were recognized as mines which the Mexicans had planted. Fear began to sweep through the whole American army.

A long call echoed down the lines for Colonel Calloway. He answered and was told that Pillow was injured and

199

wanted him at once. Without concern for his own safety the old colonel sprang to his feet and plunged blindly down the hill to the shelter where Pillow was lying on his back. His ankle had been broken by a glancing grapeshot.

"Get a message to Worth quickly!" Pillow cried half-rising on his elbow. "Tell him to bring up a brigade at once. Tell him unless we have reinforcements instantly all is lost. Maybe Franklin Pierce's brigade can be spared!"

The old colonel fumbled in his mind with the message. He was sure that Pillow wanted the whole divsion to be brought forward to relieve the storming party and wrote the request that way. He handed it to Raphael Semmes, a young navy Lieutenant, who delivered it to Worth.

The lull was broken by the unexpected arrival of the ladders, and Pillow ordered the columns to continue the attack. The troops laid the ladders against the walls and started climbing. Then all distinction between commands became lost. Lieutenant Longstreet, who was carrying the Ninth's colors, was wounded and Pickett seized them from the ground to rush up the ladder in attack. What followed was a glaring confusion to Calloway as the brilliant flags and sparkle of arms crowded across the moat.

The first ladders were thrown back by the enemy but more took their place, side by side, and fifty men went up abreast. The blue voltigeur flag, torn with shot, was planted on the parapet as a tide of Americans overflowed into the castle and took possession of the terrace within minutes.

Shortly Quitman's troops screamed into the enclosure to join the attack which was clustered about the southwest corner of the palace walls. They scaled the walls and drove into the Mexican lines, but the foe stood with unusual firmness behind their batteries and positions, and for a few minutes the fight was a hand-to-hand combat with swords, bayonets and rifle clubbing. But the resistance crumbled in face of the Americans' desperate fight to gain a foothold within the

200

palace grounds. They swarmed over the gate, despite the heavy musket fire from the windows and roofs of the castle.

Calloway found the fight was savage. The Americans showed more ferocity than ever before exhibited. The memory of the wounded Americans slaughtered by the Mexicans on the battlefield at Molino del Rey was still fresh in the attacker's mind, and quarters were rarely given.

Exhausted he dropped back to rest momentarily and took a drink from his canteen. Blake ran past toward the castle, and Calloway raised his hand to stop the lieutenant, but was interrupted by the arrival of his aide.

"Colonel," Douglas said striding up swiftly. "Something has happened."

Calloway looked at his aide's pale face wondering. "What is it, Douglas?"

"It's about that message you sent for General Pillow. It was wrong. The general asked for a brigade from Worth's division, but you must have misunderstood and asked for a whole division."

"You sure?" he asked hoarsely hardly conscious of the battle swirling around them.

"I just came from headquarters command. General Scott's hopping mad about that request. Says Pillow's a fool for making that sort of an appeal when his position didn't warrant it. Swears he'll make an investigation!"

Calloway's heart hammered with fear for Scott would nail him to the cross when the truth was learned.

Blake learned that his scouts were scattered throughout the castle during the confusion of the fight. He raced through the corridors, stumbling over bodies, calling his men to rally. He was fearful they would be drawn into a trap. But his search seemed to be in vain for they had completely disappeared from the isolated actions where the Mexicans were being slaughtered by the enraged Yanks.

He soon found the scouts in a distant section of the castle where they had cornered a small group of Mexican cadets. The cadets were boys between the ages of fourteen and sixteen, clad in gray uniforms and gaily tasseled blue caps of the National War Academy located in the castle of Chapultepec. Santa Anna had ordered the whole student body to make a stand with the Mexican troops.

The scouts, under McQuillen, were cutting up the cadets with knives and bayonets. "Clean 'em out!" he roared lifting his bayonet and charging a youth who was trying to defend himself with a rifle.

As the scouts pounded into the fight Blake raced forward to stop the slaughter that began with the screams of the dying cadets. It was the sound of a mare giving birth to a colt in the night. The horror and fatigue of five days' steady fighting was too much for Blake, but what met his sight was beyond the conception of his senses. A young Mexican lad, hardly fourteen, was pinned against the wall with the sergeant's bayonet thrust through his midriff.

The boy's eyes were briefly like those of a pleading fawn just as McQuillen ripped his bloody bayonet out and savagely rammed it again into the boy. The scream ended abruptly.

The fury in Blake's brain blinded him. He snatched up a rifle and charged the scouts yelling to halt. The bloody scene nauseated him. They were beasts with lust in their blood for killing, tramps from the streets and fields of America who had nothing better to do.

The fight swooped around him and another Mexican boy went down under a bayonet thrust, hanging to the steel, trying to pull himself loose.

Blake fired at the ceiling. The shot took effect for Campbell heard and pulled back. The others followed, pulling away from the fray. All but McQuillen had stopped and

202

were looking to Blake for orders. The big sergeant seemed fascinated by a small, terrified boy crouching against the wall.

He didn't hear Blake's shout. He circled the boy with a bloody knife. He was completely hypnotized by the boy who stared at him with fearful, black eyes.

Blake hardly knew what followed. A red mist covered his vision as he advanced swiftly across the room at McQuillen. The sergeant was like an animal instinctively sensing danger for he wheeled, saw Blake coming at him with an upraised bayonet. He tried to parry the thrust but the bayonet knocked down his guard, and entered the pit of his stomach with a smooth thrust. The charge carried Blake completely over the falling body.

McQuillen's heavy, scarred face was lighted with surprise as he pulled himself to his knees and worked with both hands to loosen the bayonet. Failing to do this he turned his eyes in a hateful glare at Blake, then crashed backward against the floor.

Blake stared numbly at the dead man, then finally a tiny stirring in his brain made him aware of what happened. He shook himself hard and walked over to stand by the Mexican boy who looked up at him blankly. Perspiration rolled down the sides of Blake's face. His limbs shook hard.

Blake turned to Williams. "Take him to camp and hold him. You're personally responsible for his safety."

Williams took the boy by the arm and half dragged him through the door. Blake leaned against the wall wiping his face, now consciously aware of the seriousness of the situation. He had killed his own sergeant in order to save an enemy's life.

He looked at the scouts now gathered in a half-circle around him, staring at him with wide, dull eyes that said nothing. His glance went to McQuillen's body, a grotesque lump of raw flesh.

Finally he spoke. "Pick up the body and take it to camp for burial. Arnold, you're in charge now!"

He walked away followed by the other scouts who were not detailed to help with the transportation of the sergeant's corpse, wondering which one of them would report this, or who would make charges against him.

There was hardly a man in his scouts who didn't hate him with a passion akin to murder itself.

Chapter Fourteen

When the scouts arrived at camp Blake ordered them to take the sergeant's body to the burial center. He reported to headquarters where he wrote out an account of McQuillen's death but filed it without reading back the report. The staff command was too busy with details of Scott's orders to keep pushing the troops directly toward the Mexican capital, where severe fighting was taking place, to notice the report.

Blake received orders to take charge of a detail rounding up the prisoners of war, captured ordnances and stores. He proceeded wearily to carry out the duties while occasionally watching, in the distance, the American troops advancing into the city through the wide, solid causeways, well elevated above the marshes.

He could look down at the whole valley of Mexico from these heights. The great wall of rugged mountains closed in from the west, and two vast, snowy peaks guarded the portals on the east. The mountains gradually subsided into verdant hills and a wide plain with varied hues where broad lakes gleamed like silver in the hot sunlight. There in the middle of the valley sat the city of Mexico, its roofs and towers black with people, and beyond were the Halls of Montezuma. However, between them and the advancing Americans stood breastworks, redoubts, cannons and a Mexican army still intact.

Blake got some of the prisoners into a rude military column as others appeared voluntarily surrendering. They joined the formation spreading the scouts so thinly that the Americans could hardly tell if any prisoners carried small arms.

"We have to take 'em back to Tacubaya tonight?" Arnold asked disgustedly.

Blake replied. "Yes. We have to nurse them until staff command relieves us."

Late in the afternoon a sergeant from Company A, whom Blake knew slightly, encountered him at the prisoner's compound. "Lieutenant," he said. "I was on messenger duty today at the general's headquarters. Overheard something about you being said. With your permission I'll tell you, but please don't say where it came from. I could get into trouble."

"I'll respect your confidence, Sergeant," he said instinctively guessing what the man had to say.

"I overheard that one of the officers in the Eleventh has placed a charge against you, sir," he said hesitatingly.

"I knew that was coming," Blake replied.

The sergeant looked away at the prisoners with the torrid sun beating across his face, half hidden under a field cap. It was a rugged, unpleasant face under any condition. "It's none of my business to tell you this, sir, but it's a charge of killing McQuillen."

The words sank into Blake's mind. He became conscious of a tree limb that made a path of shade across his feet, then lifted his eyes and glanced quietly at the prisoners standing desolately in the glare. The tiny Mexican youth was squatting near a hitching post with the horror of his experience still written across his countenance. He was a lonely, forlorn figure.

Blake was thinking. The prisoners were nothing. Just more peons conscripted from the great haciendas about the Valley of Mexico. They were the slaves of the wealthy

206

landowners forced to fight for something they did not even understand. Half-Mexican, half-negro and perhaps a tiny bit of Spanish or Indian made up their blood. He thought they looked like cattle waiting to be led to the slaughter.

The prisoners did not surrender because they lacked fight, they didn't have any enthusiasm to battle. This was not their quarrel. It was Santa Anna's war, and that of his military caste, against the north. Nobody wanted this war. His gaze shifted back to the boy again, and concluded that the lad was different from the other prisoners.

The sergeant moved his feet. "Well, that's all, Lieutenant. I ought to be getting back to my company. They'll have a muster soon. Good luck, sir!"

"Thanks, Kacey," Blake said soberly. "But why did you do this? Enlisted men don't ever take the trouble to do this sort of thing. It might get you in hot water."

The sergeant lifted gaze again and stared hotly at Blake. "I'm right proud you did it, sir," he said hoarsely. "Everybody hated McQuillen. He was a bully and a two-faced murderer. And I want you to know that the guys in my company believe in you!"

With that he wheeled away, then back again. "And if you hadn't killed him, somebody else would have!"

Blake heard somebody calling his name and turned to see the old colonel of the Eleventh leaning over the rail of the prisoner's compound. He walked across wondering at the drawn lines on the officer's countenance. No doubt it was battle fatigue.

"You heard the news?" Colonel Calloway asked harshly. Surprise washed through Blake for the colonel was normally tough but never harsh. "I'm in trouble, Blake. Serious trouble. Charges have been preferred against me."

Blake looked at him with concern. "You? What's wrong, Colonel?"

"Pillow blames me for a request he had me send Worth," he said bitterly. "Claims he sent for a brigade to be pulled up when we broke down on the scaling operations at the fosse, and that I fumbled the order and jeopardized the whole plan.

"Pillow was wounded in the foot and called me to get a message to Worth for the brigade to support us. He shifted the responsibility of the breakdown of the scaling to me and says I balled up everything. Luckily, headquarters didn't pay any attention to that message and sent Clarke's brigade instead, but it wasn't needed. Army politics! That's what it is! Scott will use this against me!"

Blake stared silently at his superior officer.

Smiling sickeningly Calloway continued. "I got the orders and sent for a whole division. That made Pillow look sick! This means I might be broken to a major or a captain. Pretty hard to take after all these years in the service. Maybe I'm the guy who'll get the firing squad. Ain't much to live for, Blake, with my wife gone and Fortune killed by a Mex's bullet. I wanted her badly to settle down and have a family. Seems like this war hasn't turned out so good for anybody but Scott and Santa Anna!"

Blake's glance swept across the beautiful valley where the golden fields of grain rippled in the soft wind. Cottages and villas were half-hidden in the foliage, and the converging roads, lined with trees, became penciled lines fading out in the twilight. "I'm in trouble too," he said hoarsely. "I'm going to get shot for doing the army a favor."

Calloway took off his hat and wiped the sweat off his forehead with a sleeve. "You stuck a long knife in McQuillen? Did the heat make you loco?"

"He was cutting up a bunch of Mexican kids," Blake spoke desperately. "See that one over there? He's the only survivor of the attack, and was about to be killed when I stabbed McQuillen."

208

Calloway glanced at the boy huddled in the corner of the fence. "Cadets from the National War College!" he said in surprise. "Nothing but a bunch of kids. What were they doing there?"

Santa Anna ordered them to make a stand with the regular Mexican troops. The boy says they were ordered back by General Bravo but refused."

"They chose to stay!" Calloway declared emphatically. "Then that makes them combatants. This ain't good, Blake. You made a bad mistake."

Blake's eyes became a hot, yellow flame. "I know but when I saw my men cutting those kids to pieces with the bayonet, that was it. I ordered them to stop and they all did, but McQuillen. He wouldn't listen! He was in the act of murdering that kid, who didn't even have a weapon!"

"What happened then?"

Blake said quietly. "I stuck him with a bayonet!"

The old man's eyes got hard. "You're going to get the book thrown at you, Blake. I'd say give you a medal, for I'm certain that it was McQuillen who murdered Fortune. An investigation showed he was absent from camp at the time of her death. He'd pled sick and you had him on discipline but he was gone from camp at that particular time of day. I figured he was out to get you but missed and hit her. He was seen riding into camp with a musket in his hand."

A surge of frustrated anger rushed through Blake. It was a delayed reaction to his troubles. "Fortune went with me that day because she loved me," he said. "She confessed her love for me and we would have been married. I'm sure it was McQuillen who fired that shot. Williams told me that he thought it was the sergeant seen riding away from the ambush!"

"I reckon killing wasn't too good for him," the old man muttered.

"I don't regret it, sir!"

The colonel clapped a hand on Blake's shoulder. "There isn't anything that I wouldn't like to do for you but right

209

now things are awful tight for me."

Blake stared at the old man for a long time. "Look, Colonel," he said sharply. "There's one thing you could do for me that would help us both. Write the letter I asked you to do about the mixup in orders at Lake Royal."

The old man turned white. He beat his fists helplessly against the rail. "I can't, Blake. There's too much at stake this time!"

"You have sacrificed my service career," Blake said angrily. "And perhaps my life to save your reputation."

Without waiting for an answer Blake wheeled and stalked off his brain numb from the fire rushing through it.

Blake was confined to his tent under technical arrest. Absently he tidied up his mess kit as his cigar ashes fell on the earth. He was thinking that the confinement of himself to the tent oppressed him more than the idea of the forthcoming trial.

Only one note which would seem encouraging to him came the previous evening when Burkhart, the bugler, told him about McQuillen's crime at Vera Cruz and offered to appear at the trial and give the court the story of the brutality and killing.

Blake mentally rehashed his life many times since his confinement. But there was still something he couldn't put his finger on. Was it the unbending regulations of the army? No, it wasn't that. It was something else, that something which was far from his understanding. That something which was so elusive his mind wouldn't grasp it.

The army regulations were so strong, so rock-bound and unbending that they seemed like ropes which dragged down every man in the service. Blake thought of them as laws which could not be broken except for the glory of killing.

Generals like Scott and Taylor and others were nothing more than dictators within their own rights. Away from Washington City they could do and act as they pleased. They could promote or hang a man. They made the law. To every man in service the generals seemed higher than God.

Now the conquest of Mexico was over. That day at sunrise delegates from the city government presented themselves to Scott, under white flags, and gave the news that Santa Anna and some of his army, still intact, had retreated toward Guadalupe Hidalgo. Icy in manner Scott immediately demanded and received the surrender of the city.

A battalion of United States Marines marched into the city, in advance of the army, and drove the looters out of the National Palace, then hoisted the Stars and Stripes. Scott dressed in full uniform and riding a white charger, with his staff and escort, halted in the middle of the great plaza and dramatically announced the completion of the conquest of Mexico.

A sound in the night disturbed Blake and for a moment he stood completely still in the center of the tent listening. His pose was that which would have been recognized by those who served under him. His right hand pulled at his ear, and his lower lip sucked in. Without thinking he raised the flap of the tent curtain, then gave a start.

Peddar Zaskq walked into the canvas space with blue shining eyes. He seated himself upon a wooden box and spoke. "You're in great trouble, Captain."

"Then you have heard?" Blake asked.

"The sergeant deserved his fate."

Blake said sharply, "I might be hung!"

"Yes, that is true, señor!"

"Let me assure you that Sarita is safe in her secret with me. I will never reveal you or her to the army authorities for using me as a tool for spying." Blake spoke in a close whisper.

211

Zaskq lifted his head and stared at Blake with wide blue eyes that were fathomless as the ocean. It gave Blake a feeling as if he were sinking deeper into a void world, into the great beyond. He felt as though this man was holding him in some mysterious power, perhaps hypnotism.

He said sadly. "It distresses me for you to talk that way, Blake. You're so mistaken, for we are not members of any spy ring. As for McQuillen, if he were alive, I might strangle him with my own hands. It was he who ambushed you that day and killed Fortune."

Blake looked at him in amazement. "I guessed it was McQuillen. But tell me, Zaskq, why have you come back?"

"I came for the boy you saved at Chapultepec," he said gently. "There is nothing to stop me. He is the son of Don Romero whom you visited at Saltillo. He has already been spirited from the prison compound and will be taken to Juquila for safekeeping."

He paused. "There have been terrible happenings in the city. Santa Anna released two thousand criminals from the city jails and while the Yanks were in the process of organizing their occupation of the city sniping began from rooftops and windows.

"Colonel Garland was shot in the outbreak and trouble started. The americanos broke into houses, cantinas and shops. The strife became worse, women joining in, and unarmed people took to throwing stones and furniture from the windows. Soon the Yankee troops were indulging in drinking and looting.

"The disasters which have marked these last few days have been horrible. The nights are dark and fearful. Dead bodies lay scattered throughout the streets. In all streets which are occupied by the Americans the people fight boldly and with fury. Most of them engage without firearms. Even in the midst of combat the Americans are given up to most infamous outrages, and General Scott has threatened to level the whole city if the Mexicans don't stop!"

"Sarita?" Blake asked numbly. "Was she caught in this outrage?"

"I don't know where she is," Zaskq replied in a tight voice. "She was captured by some of Santa Anna's military police after the battle of Molino del Rey. We haven't found any traces of her yet!"

Blake seized the guide by the shoulders. "You fool!" he cried shaking him roughly. "You've let her die in Santa Anna's hands!"

Zaskq disengaged himself. "She's too valuable for him to kill. Santa Anna would like to use her to make Juquila raise an army for her release. Now I must go!"

"I will go with you!" Blake said savagely reaching for his jacket.

Zaskq swung back facing him firmly. "You must wait! If I locate her then you can come!"

Blake nodded slowly. If he left the army now under any condition the charges against him about helping the enemy would be strengthened.

Major Elijah Calloway, former commandant of the Eleventh Regiment, walked slowly back to his tent after the final session of the court-martial of Lieutenant Jed Blake.

He was too sick at heart to take notice of the fierce sunlight for Blake had been sentenced to be hung on the 28th day of September, 1847, for the killing of his Sergeant Barney McQuillen during the battle of Chapultepec.

Maury Williams, the Texas scout, was the only witness to speak out for Blake at the court-martial. The other scouts seemed to have their words twisted by the defense counsel of the court. Even Burkhart, the bugler, tried to tell some bloody tale about McQuillen at Vera Cruz but was cut short and dismissed from the witness stand.

213

His own testimony in Blake's behalf was not strong enough. Time and again he tried to speak out for his former scout only to be stung into humiliation by having his testimony turned into a defense of himself.

Calloway had had a court-martial a week previously which stripped him of his rank and reduced him to a major without command. He now awaited transportation back to the states. He knew what this meant for the army would retire him without honors, and he would spend the remaining years a lonely old man. The service to which he had given his whole life was throwing him out. He was the scapegoat for the staff command's mistake at Chapultepec when the storming assault broke down and many American lives were uselessly lost.

He poured himself a drink of water and dropped wearily into the plain wooden chair which had been nailed together out of barrel staves and other lumber scraps. The weather was miserably hot and perspiration poured off his lean jaws.

His thoughts rambled briefly over his past. His life was a failure in the army. He was a brilliant young officer who had bad breaks. Taylor had twice reprimanded him during the Black Hawk campaign and the Florida war with its frightful calamity at Lake Royal, where Blake was unjustly accused, had played havoc with his reputation among the high-ranking officers.

He reached into his war chest and took out a revolver and studied it with a furrowed brow. The gun was a deadly, shining instrument made for killing. He wondered if it would be good to join Mary again. None of this would have happened if she had been with him. Her wonderful counsel and love would have helped take care of his problems. Fortune had given him some satisfaction but as soon as she was gone troubles piled up hurriedly.

Somebody walked up to the curtain flaps and rustled them. Looking up Calloway called for his former aide, Lieutenant Douglas, to enter.

214

The young officer pulled back the tent flaps and came in a forlorn, pathetic figure with a distressed light in his eyes. Calloway studied him briefly thinking that here was a fresh, arrogant kid growing up in the service, much like himself twenty years ago, and making mistake after mistake, but not admitting them. Something was going to stop him sooner or later.

"Glad to have found you in, sir," Douglas said nervously.

"What is it you want?" Calloway asked gruffly.

After a long pause, penetrated heavily with a foreboding air, the boy said. "I'm in trouble sir. Bad trouble!"

"What kind of trouble you in?"

The boy whispered trembling, "It's about the scouts of the Eleventh, sir!"

"Go see Colonel Howe," Calloway replied. "He's taken over the Eleventh. I've been relieved of duty!"

"But I thought you might help me," Douglas said tearfully.

Calloway asked curiously. "What about the scouts?"

"They're dead, sir!" Douglas whispered his eyes glowing feverishly. "Gray ran them into an ambushed battery in the city. All were wiped out but Williams!"

The words got into Calloway's brain and wound around like small worms crawling through the tissue. Suddenly they struck him like a physical blow and brought him swiftly to his feet. "My God!" he swore loudly.

The boy stared dully at the gun in Calloway's hand. The old man laid it on the war chest and stood back wiping his face with the back of his hand. "What happened?" he asked hoarsely.

The boy explained in a trembling voice, shifting his feet, uncomfortably under Calloway's burning gaze. When he finished the old officer demanded. "What's it got to do with you?"

"As aide for Colonel Howe," he choked and tears ran down his cheeks. "I got the orders for the scouts to

215

reconnaissance the area to the southeast of the city, but I mixed them and sent the scouts in the opposite direction where they were trapped and wiped out!"

Suddenly Calloway threw back his head and roared with laughter. He stopped quickly and looked at the dismayed young man. "I couldn't help it, Lieutenant. It is a familiar story. Fate works in funny ways. Just like my own career!"

"I don't understand," Douglas muttered.

Calloway said, "You want me to intercede for you with Colonel Howe?"

The boy nodded humbly.

Calloway smiled grimly. "My word isn't worth anything, Lieutenant. I've been stripped of my rank and being shipped back to the states to be retired."

"Please see Colonel Howe," Douglas pleaded. "You can give me a character reference for service under you."

"Lieutenant!" Calloway chuckled mirthlessly. "You're finding out the facts of life. Nobody is going to help you now. You've made your own bed and you'll sleep in it, but be a man and take it on the chin. Get some guts, stand up to your problems."

"I can't!" the young officer wailed. "Everybody at the headquarters knows about this and I've become ostracized!"

Calloway said bluntly. "I can't help you. My hands are tied. I can only advise you to face your troubles regardless of the cost.

"I know of only one man in this army who has courage. It's Jed Blake. He's had the guts to openly speak his mind about this war being a political maneuver for Polk and his mealy-mouthed gang of office seekers. He has suffered wrong throughout his army career because of his honesty and courage.

"He has been called yellow, a traitor and it was even said he killed his own brother, but I was indirectly responsible for that, because my pride wouldn't let me change the order he protested against. Some even hold him responsible for

216

Fortune's death. And those who have wronged him most have been the ones to yell the loudest for his scalp.

"This is good-bye and good luck, Lieutenant!"

The boy blinked quickly, then realized that his argument was futile and swung to leave the tent without saluting. Calloway stared briefly at the flapping curtains.

There was nothing he could do for Douglas. Calloway realized that twenty years ago he had been in the same situation but the problem lay within himself. It would be interesting to wait and watch, but there was no time left for him; the sands of time were running out fast.

He picked up a pen, drew some paper from his table and wrote rapidly. This letter to the War Department would clear Blake's record in the Seminole War. After finishing he put down the pen and let his glance travel slowly across the table to the gun. He reached for it and checked the chamber to see if it was loaded. He lifted the gun thinking of his wife and Fortune.

The roar shattered the silence, spreading out in waves over the camp, across the Valley of Mexico disturbing the vultures perched in high branches. They flapped away on slow, awkward wings, toward the tall, white-capped mountains against the horizon.

Blake put his head out of the tent and asked the guard the cause of the disturbance. The sentry stopped and half-turned. "I reckon somebody fired off his pistol accidently," he said.

Blake ate his supper in the tent that night, then walked around the restricted area for exercise. He looked down from the heights at the fires of the army camp on the hillside, twinkling like fireflies. Each was a tiny jewel in itself, while overhead the stars reflected the radiance of the leaping flames.

The American army was now in possession of the city of Mexico. He asked himself if he understood the war against disease, sickness, guns, rapine, murder, and fire. But he couldn't answer, nor could he comprehend, for his training was only in the art of killing, and the many ways to subject the conquered.

Calloway was dead! The news of the old officer's suicide hardly shocked his already heavy state of affliction. Nothing mattered anymore for soon he would be dead. God had made it this way!

He shook his head. He didn't understand God; of course not, how could he in his limited capacity for understanding? His thoughts lived in the stillness of the night and he seemed to feel something greater than himself stirring around him. Death had followed the army from Palo Alto, Resaca de la Palma, Monterrey, Vera Cruz, Cerro Gordo, Molino del Rey, Chapultepec and Mexico City. Many had died and now it was his turn.

Footsteps approaching turned him to find Maury Williams coming out of the soft, velvet darkness. The scout nodded and paused to light a cigar before speaking. "Reckon I got time to make a speech before the sentry gets back around," he said softly. "Thought I'd better come and give you the news, Lieutenant."

"What news, Williams?" Blake's voice was hardly audible for he sensed something dreadful.

After awhile Williams spoke again. "I am the only living member of the scouts, sir."

Heavy thoughts hammered in Blake's head. "What's happened?" he whispered.

Williams replied in a low voice. "They were wiped out in the city, in the Calle San Juan. Lieutenant Gray was put in charge right after your arrest. We were with Worth's advance columns marching into the city. Gray didn't know how to spread his men in Indian fashion. He got orders to turn into the southeast area for some reason, and he ran us

218

completely into a Mexican battery before we knew what had happened!"

Blake put his hands up to his face and wiped it clean from the hot perspiration rolling down his gaunt cheeks. All the scouts were gone except this quiet, slim man at his side. Michaels, the hulking boy with the light colored eyes who wanted nothing more than a few pieces of gold coins to take home. Hultkrans, the eagle-beaked Tennesseean who had shifted to the scouts because the infantry wanted to be rid of him. Campbell, scion of a wealthy family cut off from his inheritance. Bush with his ungainly body, ill-length arms and legs. Arnold, the fat jolly one. Ichler, the Jew. Young Jack Burkhart, barely eighteen, and others. They were dead, a parade of faces marching across his mind.

"I hope it was easy for them," he said without feeling, as his thoughts passed on to Warren, McQuillen and Fortune Calloway, then Dennis; yes Dennis, big, blundering and arrogant. Finally to Henry.

"I don't think any of them suffered," Williams said. "Maybe the kid. When the grape hit us I was lucky to be off on the right flank, the only one to be away. Gray had the scouts bunched like bees. I refused to stay in that formation."

"You say the bugler suffered?" Blake asked wide-eyed.

Williams nodded. "The shot knocked him off his horse, and the Mexicans finished him with a bayonet. They worked on every scout to be sure they were all dead!"

"Merciful God!" Blake whispered trembling.

"Easy, Lieutenant," Williams said. "This wasn't easy to tell you. But the news might have got to you some other way and not as good as I told you!"

"Thanks, Williams. Now you'd better go before the sentry gets back on his round and finds you here. He will report you."

Williams leaned closer. "Look, Lieutenant," he whispered. "I can help you escape. There's a way of getting out of camp. You can make your way north to the border and go to my place in Texas. You can change your name and live there the rest of your life in peace. Some of the troopers will help get you out of camp."

Blake put a hand on the scout's shoulder. "You're a real friend, Williams. But I can't leave now. I have to face that hangman's rope. Maybe everything will turn out all right. so long!"

Chapter Fifteen

Blake was aroused from a deep slumber by some vague
sound outside his tent. Wide-eyed he stared into the
dark gloom gathered about the interior of his canvas shelter.
His life in the army had trained him to arouse himself
instantly at the slightest sound, or the smallest impression of
danger.

The familiar sounds of the sleeping army gradually came
into his consciousness. The thumping of hooves in the
nearby corral drowned out the call of sentries from their out-
posts, and the low muted voices of soldiers passing his tent
became more audible with his mind passing into active
thought.

The wind softly flapped the tent curtain and the moon rising over the snow summit of Popocatepetl lighted the right
side of the tent. The impression was a focus of awareness, a
sensation beyond his senses, and the experience of reaching
out into infinite space, beyond the stars. A blinding light
seemed to wrap around him painfully searing him.

Sitting up quietly on the side of the blanket he reached for
his boots and slid into them, so as not to let go of that feeling within himself. He saw clearly the futility of all he had
done in peace and war. He had been dehumanized, selfish,
blind and for what purpose? In groping to find the answer
and its folly he saw his own absurdness. His execution

221

would mean nothing to the world for he was an instrument of war, a machine made to kill, a destructive force.

The moonlight became a lovely vivid pattern of glory against the wall of his tent. Its beauty held his attention until he felt completely a part of everything including the moonlight and shadows. The whispering of the winds in the trees was his own voice speaking out and the sounds of the camp blending into one harmonious melody.

He would die at dawn by hanging, a penalty for killing his own sergeant at Chapultepec. If Williams would come again tonight and ask if he could escape to Texas and live the remainder of his life, he would not refuse.

Colonel Wilson Peck of headquarters staff, led the attack on him at the court martial with Williams testifying in his behalf but admitted under oath that he had witnessed Blake bayonet the sergeant. The other scouts attested against their former officer, referring time and again to his conduct in the field. The bugler tried to reveal McQuillen's bloody act at Vera Cruz but was blocked by the defense counsel. Calloway slipped badly in his testimony and the decision rendered was a sentence of death by hanging, at dawn, September 28, 1847.

The sentence came as a surprise to Blake's fellow officers, Jackson, Grant, Lee, Hitchcock, Longstreet, Semmes, Pickett and others, for he had a brilliant record as a scout in the United States Army and his family was traditionally military and strongly entrenched with the administration.

Sergeant Barney McQuillen's death was of little concern to the army. It was a welcome to all, for the bloodthirsty noncom had caused trouble for most of the officers and men. But it was the murder of Fortune Calloway, whom many believed Blake had killed in outright jealousy, that invoked the wrath of the troops against him and eventually brought the sentence of death upon his head.

Violence and disaster had laid its heavy hand upon the troops and fellow officers of Blake's old regiment. Gone was Wiley, the fighting devil who had stormed the castle of

Chapultepec, single-handedly destroying a nest of Mexican sharpshooters. Warren slept in a shallow grave, and Henry and Fortune were together, at least in spirit. The old colonel had killed himself in shame and disgrace.

Now in this long moment he could see the loss of life, destruction and the bloody battles, pain, hunger and cruelty that went with the nature of war. The glory march which began at Corpus Christi left the scattered bones of his American brethren lying in the marshlands, across the deserts, on the high mountain slopes and half-buried in the streams and lakes of Mexico.

The purpose of the death of those strong, brave souls who had served with him through the long Mexican campaign of 1846–47 was now revealed. He didn't want to die, but as an instrument of war and politics, he, Jed Blake, had lived a useless and futile life and there was no further purpose for which to live.

The guard passed the tent, feet thudding wearily against the dry earth and faded into the night. Without warning the shadow of a man suddenly silhouetted against the outside tent wall in the moonlight. There was the tiny sound of a knife blade puncturing the canvas and slowly ripping away the barrier between him and the night. He was thinking that Williams had returned.

Moonlight flooded the tent, like a great golden pool flashing upon the knife blade, in the hand of the man who was squatting there. Out of the night came a soft whisper calling his name. Then a long silence and it came again. He hardly heard because of the loud beating of his heart.

"Blake? Are you there?" Zaskq's voice whispered. "I see you. Come quickly. Hurry while the guard has gone for water."

Blake stepped quickly through the gaping hole and crouched beside the guide. "The other guard?" He muttered. "He should be here!"

"Yes, Lieutenant. He is out of our way temporarily. I've horses hidden behind the shelter of the rocks over there."

"Why are you doing this, Zaskq?" Blake whispered.

"To repay my debt. Remember, I promised!"

"Blake said grimly. "I can't go with you. I've also a debt to pay to my people. It would be cowardly for me to run away now."

"You are right," the guide replied. "But Sarita needs you. I've found where she is being held. She will die unless we hurry. I haven't time to get help from others."

A great urgency whirled through Blake's brain. He motioned for the guide to lead the way. They half-ran across the space of moonlight into the woods. Here they paused for a moment then hurried through the high weeds to a long ravine, passing the campfires and sleeping soldiers, Zaskq swiftly led the way into the moonlight and darkness of the scrub pines where a pair of horses stood quietly.

Peddar Zaskq put a hand over the horse's muzzle and cautiously guided it through the woods with Blake following. They passed silently through the sentry lines without being challenged, then stopped and mounted. Just as they rode off a shot followed by shouts was heard in the distant camp.

Zaskq put spurs to his horse's flanks and dashed off into the silvery night. "Hurry!" he cried. "They have found you gone. Soon they will be sending riders in every direction. We must be far ahead of them by dawn!"

Blake rode blindly through the darkness holding his head down to protect his eyes against the whipping mane. He asked himself silently. What did all this mean? Was Zaskq leading him into a trap to kill him?

His heart pounded fiercely with the rhythmic beat of hooves against the hard earth. The chilly night air pierced his flesh until he wondered if all this suffering would bring death without further complications. His life had always been one of extreme danger, of pursuit and being pursued. This was just another phase of his life. He was riding out of his past into a dark, unknown future in this mysterious Mexico—the land of the ancient gods.

Now down through the valley they rode swiftly and up a steep slope where the trees threw dark shadows against the rocks. Zaskq signaled for Blake to pull up. They dismounted, together, and listened for sounds of pursuit.

"We are now safe from the Americans," the scout said. "They will look around the city for you before starting into the countryside. It will be dawn before they can locate the tracks of our horses and by that time we will have Sarita and be at the monastery at Chizza. They will not venture there; however, I will plan our escape so they will think that you have been murdered by the banditti!"

Blake said firmly. "I will return to my camp as quickly as Sarita is freed from Santa Anna's gang!"

"We will wait on that decision, Blake," Zaskq remarked. "Meanwhile, I must be honest with you. Your fate is in Sarita's hands. You will have the choice of staying with us or leaving. If she rejects you, then you are free to return to your army to die in dishonor."

The tall American said gravely, "Let us wait until Sarita is safely established in her own home. But meanwhile you'd better let me borrow one of those guns in your belt. I won't use it on you!"

Zaskq laughed quietly. "I have little fear of you shooting me. You are too honest. Besides you're in love with Sarita!"

It seemed to Blake that they were an exceedingly long time in reaching their destination. Peddar Zaskq halted in a

225

wooded, moonlit area and dismounted. They tied their horses to a clump of brush and proceeded to the edge of the knoll which overlooked a sleeping village.

The guide moved swiftly to the left of the village in long strides. Blake followed, his heart pumping loudly, wondering where they were going. Soon he discovered that they were moving toward an hacienda, half-hidden in a small, dark grove of trees.

They stopped and surveyed the buildings where Blake saw a lone sentry pacing the patio in the deep shadows. Zaskq signaled for Blake to wait and sinking back in the shadows of the trees he watched the guide. Silently, Zaskq crept down upon the guard, like a panther stalking its victim. There was a leap, a brief struggle, and the moonlight flashed on the sentry's face on the floor.

The guide stood up and waved to Blake. The American joined him, and together, they moved on silent feet toward a door. Zaskq gently pushed it back. Beyond the threshold was a long hall shrouded in darkness where a guttered candle on a table flickered its lemon-yellowish light faintly over the gloomy rafters and walls. They moved inside and closed the door, then stood there.

To their right was an enormous room where five Mexicans sat around a table playing cards. The man who sat facing the door was a sandy bearded individual with heavy eyebrows. Zaskq's breath came in a soft hissing sound. "Zapatos!" he muttered. "We must work fast. Follow me!"

He stepped into the room while Blake stationed himself at the door to prevent any surprise attack. The card players looked up in amazement, threw down their cards and rose with their hands high as Zaskq backed them against the wall. He quickly disarmed them and motioned for the gaudy uniformed officer to step forward.

"Where's Señorita Gonzales?" Zaskq demanded thrusting a gun barrel under the officer's nose.

"I don't understand you, señor," the colonel smiled suavely.

Blake became almost paralyzed with fear at what he saw. Zaskq pulled a knife from his belt and slowly and deliberately pushed past Zapatos to the first man. He thrust the blade against the Mexican's throat. The soldier blanched and cringed. "Where is she?" he demanded again.

The soldier's underjaw worked noisely, then his whisper became audible, "Sobre, Señor!" he pointed to the ceiling and broke into a swift mixture of Tuscan and Spanish.

Zaskq called to Blake. "Upstairs to the left. First room. Go quickly! Be careful for she is hurt!"

Blake went up the stairs fast, his heart pounding heavily and felt his way along the gloomy hallway. He found the door, lifted his gun, and kicked open the flimsy portal. A wrinkled, old crone was leaning over a rumpled bed where Sarita lay on her face, a stark, pathetic figure.

The candlelight gleamed upon her golden face. Slowly his startled eyes lighted upon the deep, angry whiplashes across her back. The surge of horror made him desperately sick.

He ran to the bed, knelt and touched her tenderly whispering her name. The old crone muttered. "It's too late, señor. She's dying!"

"What happened?" he cried.

"The officer, he tried to learn the secret place of the Holy One, but she wouldn't tell. He lashed her with the whip." she shook her gray head sadly.

"Can I move her?" he asked as hatred clouded his brain.

"It matters not where she dies, señor," the old woman shrugged.

Blake gently wrapped the girl in a dirty blanket and cradled her in his arms. She moaned a little and her eyelids fluttered long, black lashes like the incandescent wings of a butterfly over a flower. They opened and stared at him vacantly, wide, dark pools of light.

Slowly recognition came into them. Her lips moved faintly. "You came," the words hardly audible. "I knew you would. Take me home!"

Pain tore gaps in his heart. Tears almost blinded him as he made his way down the stairs with the limp body in his arms. Stopping in the doorway he looked with sorrowful eyes toward Zaskq who took a step forward eyes widening, unbelieving. His face became deadly white.

"She's dying!" Blake barely voiced his words.

Slowly, like a great serpent Peddar Zaskq turned. Blake held his breath fully aware of what was coming. Zaskq had become an angel of death. He pointed a long forefinger at the first man, then did the same at each of them. Each surprisingly slid to the floor as though dead.

He turned to the Mexican officer. Upward went his empty hand toward Zapatos' throat. The doomed man watched the hand with a ghastly fascinated stare as it hovered briefly then moved with lightning speed.

The victim's cry was cut short in a choking gurgle as blood gushed from his mouth. Zaskq watched the doomed man struggle briefly then fall across the table and roll to the floor.

He motioned Blake to follow and led the way to the horses. There in the darkness he asked Blake to lay the girl on the ground where he checked her pulse and wounds. "You will have to carry her for the rest of the night, señor," he said. "Can you do it?"

"Have you forgotten that I love her?" Blake asked.

Silently Zaskq lifted the girl and waited for Blake to mount. Then he handed her up to Blake and they rode closely through the moonlit night. With each step of the horse's hooves Blake felt that fresh pain was set in motion in the girl.

By morning they reached the edge of a blue lake whose far shores were a dim outline in the far distance of mountains that lost their heads in the sky. As ever the great twin peaks, Popocatepetl and Ixtaccihuatl pushed their silvery crests into the glowing dawn.

Dismayed at the lack of life in the girl Blake laid her upon the rude bed which Zaskq built out of pine branches.

Then the guide gathered twigs and made a fire. Afterwards he told Blake to leave them for an hour or so. "She will live," he said in reply to Blake's anxious query. "But there is much to do and you cannot witness what is to take place!"

Obediently Blake went into the woods until he was out of sight of the camp and laid down under a tree. Soon he was fast asleep. Later he awoke to find the sun well into the morning and rising he walked back to camp.

Zaskq was sitting cross-legged beside the girl. He smiled and rose to greet Blake. "Welcome, Blake," he said. "She is much better."

Blake looked down at the girl in surprise. She was weak and pale as after a hard sickness but beyond that all traces of death had disappeared. "Come and sit beside me," she spoke in her beautiful liquid voice. "I am grateful to you. Will you come to the monastery with my friend and I?"

He shook his head sadly. "I must return to the American army."

"Come to Chizza for there you will find life and love," she whispered. "I will await you there."

He looked at her wonderingly. Could he give up the past, his family, and his whole life that he knew for this strange and beautiful girl? He could escape to Texas and make a new life, but now he had to sacrifice that. As a man of peace, of hope, of alliance with the earth, and with constructive living he could start afresh with something to love and live for. The realization struck him with an emotional impact. Now he knew that this was true. He could make the change.

He leaned forward and kissed her. "Will you marry me?" he asked hoarsely.

She whispered, "If it is the will of the SUGMAD."

"I have only life and death to offer. Not life and love. I am a hunted man, to be killed on sight."

She smiled. "You are free. No one will ever find you."

"She speaks the truth," Zaskq said coming up and putting

a hand on Blake's shoulder. "I desire that you come and be my brother, and live with us."

"Yes," he murmured thinking of his decision and the life he might have had in Texas. "I will come and live with you."

"Ah," Zaskq remarked turning. "I see that the party from Chizza has arrived for you, Señorita. You and I will stay here, Blake, to see that no one follows."

A party of men and women in peon attire suddenly appeared out of the tall, waving grass at the edge of the lake. A small boy came forward to greet them. It was the lad whom Blake had saved from the sergeant's bayonet.

They lifted Sarita to her feet and carried her to the edge of the grass where she half-turned and waved to Blake then disappeared into the foliage.

Zaskq gathered sticks and built up the dying fire. He roasted some dried venison and divided it with Blake. They squatted in the shade of a large tree overlooking the lake waters and ate. A single cloud floating through the sky, a white patch against the water, made Blake remember his years of scouting in the Great Lakes region.

After eating Zaskq said, "Sarita will explain to Juquila and prepare for your coming to Chizza. Meanwhile, I must make a blind for any American pursuers by making it appear that you've been murdered by the natives. May I have your coat and cap please?"

Blake handed the garments to him. "What did you do to bring Sarita to life again? She was dying."

"Through the use of herbs and other natural means that God has provided for us. It is an ancient Indian art of healing and someday I'll teach you. Now stay here and sleep if you can. We are safe from pursuit at the present."

Blake pillowed his head against the roots of the tree and dozed for an hour or so before the guide shook him. Zaskq had brought back a wide sombrero for him. The man did not bother to explain where he had been nor did Blake ask, but noticed the horses were gone.

"We will walk for a little while now, Blake," Peddar Zask said stepping into the sunlight and through the high water weeds along the direction which the girl and her party had taken hours before. "It will be several hours before we find a way to cross the lake,"

Blake followed pulling the hat far down over his eyes to ward off the growing heat of the brilliant sunlight. Life had become a pattern of events, one growing into the other like that of checkers, fitting the pieces into a puzzle. Sorrow and happiness; pain and joy were now one, and beyond that, all flesh and spirit were separated no longer. Life, wisdom and love had become the shining ideals of his search. He had found life and hope even in the shadow of the gallows.

They walked together, side by side, through the rustling grass, Blake looking at the strange blue waters while puzzled, but calm thoughts kept running through his head. The sun rose higher in the heavens and its thick light spread over the ancient land steaming through his heavy shirt. Perspiration began to roll down the middle of his shoulder blades.

They came to a small cove on the shores of the lake where a dugout canoe was pulled hard against the white sands. To the left were cultivated fields which ran down to the shoreline. Behind, the wooded foothills marked the beginning of the Sierra mountains—long slopes rising into the low clouds.

A hardy, wrinkled old man rose from out of the roots of a thick tree and stood waiting for them. Zaskq spoke a few words in Spanish, then motioned Blake to help push the canoe off the sand and got in. They paddled the old shallow boat through the heavy grass. A light haze covered the mountains and distant shoreline, despite the intensity of the brilliant sun. Only the beating of the paddle broke the silence.

Blake dropped off into a light sleep dreaming of the girl. After awhile he awoke to find he had slept through the afternoon into early evening. The boatman was sitting in the stern, straight and tall, paddling wearily up a small inlet. A wind had sprung up chilling Blake to the bone and he pulled himself into a small huddle and looked around. Zaskq was lying in the bottom of the boat, his hat pulled over his eyes.

He lifted his hat and smiled. "We'll soon be there," he said sitting up. "It's just around the next curve."

The boat shot around a thickly wooded bend and ahead in the fading light was a landing dock and the pale white walls of the monastery. Pine trees stood like guards along the shore, their long branches swaying gracefully in the evening breeze. Bougainvillea hung in thick scarlet sheets on the walls of the house. In the distance were the huts of the peons.

The paddler skillfully guided the canoe into the dock and jumped out to hold it steady for the passengers to step ashore. "We're home, my friend," Zaskq said.

They walked up the path to the white-walled monastery where numerous candles flamed like tiny fireflies in the night. Sarita was standing in the door, dark and lovely — a bronze goddess in the faint light. Her beauty brought a gasp of delight from his lips. He hesitated, wondering if she might still be ill.

"Welcome, my beloved," she spoke in a rich, contralto voice reaching her hands out to him. "Welcome home!"

Her lips were fresh and wonderful to his hot flesh. Freeing her Blake stepped back looking anxiously into her deep, black eyes. "Are you well?" he asked hoarsely.

"Still shaky and needing rest," she replied. "Since arriving Juquila has seen that I've gotten the best of medicines and care. Otherwise I'm filled with joy that you're here!"

"I do not understand," he said puzzled. "You were dying but now you appear almost well."

232

She smiled gently saying nothing.

He asked. "We will be married?"

"Yes, I have the permission of the Holy One!"

Looking through the door at the darkening sky she spoke again. "I want it that way. Let us not be parted again."

"We will be married tomorrow at dawn," she said stepping away as her brother came into the room. "Peddar Zaskq will attend to your wants. This is your home. Use it as your own."

The youth whose life he saved at Chapultepec came out of a side door smiling at Blake and led him to an upstairs room. Outside the wind was rising as if a storm was brewing. The whole evening had a strange cast as if he was an actor in a play, or was dreaming. Was he already dead? He asked himself.

He took off his clothes in the dark room and lay down in a soft bed listening to the wind beat against the monastery wall. He thought of the old colonel and Major Dennis. The war had brought them death. Many of his comrades were sleeping in the hot sands under the ancient stars of Mexico. Someday he would go back, gather up the bones of his brother and put them with Fortune's. They would like that.

A full, round moon rising over the eastern horizon threw a yellow light across his bed. This was like another world to Blake, the murmuring of voices in the night, the wind and silence of the dark room. Gradually his whirling senses came to a halt and he slept.

The soft beating of drums and guitars aroused Blake during the hour preceding dawn. When he opened his eyes a small lamp was glowing brightly on the table beside his bed. A pair of blue velvet trousers and a sash of pure yellow silk hung over a chair. Tucked under the lamp was a note from Peddar Zaskq which told him his old clothes had been

233

burned as a token of forgetting the past, and that he was to bathe himself and put on new clothing. This was his first step into this new life.

A servant came into the room, bowed and led Blake to the adjoining compartment where he found a tub of hot water. He bathed and put on the clothes as instructed.

Peddar Zaskq came for him and silently conducted him downstairs into a side garden. The man was barefooted and dressed in a similar attire except for a blue sash around his slim waist. Blake realized this was the first time he had seen his former army guide without his customary scout's attire.

The wind suddenly swooped out of the sky and drove across the garden in a burst of life. A single drum began to beat around him and got into his heart and pounded. Then figures moved out of the morning mist toward him. He remembered this was the drum of ECK he had heard so many times during the campaign. Impossible? But it was so much like his own heartbeat.

Somewhere in the mist of the morning came a high, sweet tenor of a man's voice singing some strange, exotic melody which stirred and lifted Blake's spirit into the very heights of ecstasy.

A flame of color tipped the bough of a limb above his head, and then the whole eastern sky became a myriad pattern of glowing shades. He walked through the yard, barefooted with Zaskq, into a broad court thinking that this was the moment he was to die at the end of a rope on the gallows. Was he dreaming? Had he died and this was the dream which came to him in the grave?

Juquila, the ECK Master of the Ancient Order of Vairagi, was standing at the far end of the courtyard, beside a small flat altar on which sat a bowl of flaming fire. He watched them with dark serene eyes as he touched his right thumb to his forehead and his heart, then a warm handshake.

Then Blake saw the girl stepping into the patio, attended by the Mexican boy. The very beauty of the young Mexican

234

woman melted all finiteness within him into a great burning love, an emotion which he had never before experienced. He suddenly realized that this marriage was like the world above and the earth below consummating into the living life, the sheer mystery of ecstasy.

She was dressed in a sleeveless gown of pure white linen, with a yellow sash like his own, wrapped around her slim waist. She carried in one hand a beautiful crescent which gleamed like a shimmering rainbow in the soft colors of the dawn.

Zaskq whispered for him to take her hand and walk together toward the priest with bowed heads. With a trembling in his legs he did as directed and paused before the tall man who passed a hand over their heads and gave his blessings in an ancient Indian language. At the same moment the sun lifted its head across the horizon shooting its light into the whole world.

"Barefooted before the world, with your faces to the east, you are now joined together as one," said Juquila in soft spanish. "This is the Alpha and Omega; as the Shariyat-Ki-Sugmad says. The beginning, without ending. Eternity goes on forever and ever. And so must you, Souls, through the succession of many lives until you become perfect in God."

With this he passed his hand through the fire and pointed at the morning star blazing brightly overhead, despite the increasing light of the new day, saying, "With the morning star as the living witness I now put your feet upon the spiritual path of God to follow together, forever!"

He pressed his thumb against Blake's forehead, between the eyebrows and repeated the ritual with the girl. He said, "My daughter look into the sun and say: 'This man is the light of my world and I must look to the light at all times!'"

She lifted her lovely face repeating the words in the bright glow of the morning sun. Then the priest said to Blake. "My son, look into the dawn and say. 'This woman is my Soul and I must treat my Soul justly at all times!'"

Blake repeated the words and the priest continued while dipping his hands into a bowl of water. "This water is from heaven," he said putting his right hand upon Blake's head and his left on the girl's. "And as long as you drink of it you will never thirst. Now kneel on your right knee and look into the rising sun."

He put his hands over their eyes saying, "In darkness as well as in light you will never betray one another. You will keep your wedlock holy and filled with the light of God. Your children shall be initiated in the mystery of God, and taught that the SUGMAD is the Supreme One of all. You must constantly pray for kindness, sympathy and understanding of one another.

"You must meet on the spiritual grounds of understanding with ever opening hearts, ready to receive the other, for now as children of the day, you are beyond the plane of physical existence; beyond the realm of the mind and in the world of God. Yet you must never forget that you live in this world, but not of it.

"In the light of the morning star and the pure rays of the first sign of dawn you are joined as a perfect one; man and woman!"

The sun was over the horizon and day was beginning. The drums were softening in the distance and the singer's voice seemed far away, a faint sound like some celestial music. A steady wave of joy was rising up through him, from some unknown recess within him, deep down, far down inside him, coming evermore into his consciousness like surges of waves on an ocean beach.

"Go," said the priest in his wonderful magnetic voice. "Go for your feet are firmly planted upon the path of SUGMAD. Live in joy, peace and love. Go and prepare yourselves for life together!"

They walked through the throngs of people, through the courtyard and garden into the house, hand in hand, and up the stairs to the room.

They paused before the open window looking out at the golden red light of the sun flooding the fields and mountains. The lake was a brilliant flame of fire and from out of the mist came the singer's voice lifted in one joyous note ending in a high call which was instantly answered by the whistling birds.

Blake was in the throes of ecstasy as he looked across the mountains thinking of the American army lying beyond like a sprawling animal, of his comrades and the land of his childhood, and of his mother, none of whom he was ever to see again. But there was no sorrow in his heart for he was lifted into the realm of great joy.

The girl leaned against him and her voice came in the softest whisper. "Your life is my life; my life is your life. We shall live together in peace and joy!"

Turning he gazed into the depths of her deep, shining eyes and found himself in a burst of wondrous happiness.

INDEX

239

240

How to Study ECK Further

People want to know the secrets of life and death. In response to this need Sri Harold Klemp, today's spiritual leader of Eckankar, and Paul Twitchell, its modern-day founder, have written special monthly discourses which reveal the Spiritual Exercises of ECK—to lead Soul in a direct way to God.

Those who wish to study Eckankar can receive these special monthly discourses which give clear, simple instructions for the spiritual exercises. The first annual series of discourses is *The ECK Dream Discourses.* Mailed each month, the discourses will offer insight into your dreams and what they mean to you.

The techniques in these discourses, when practiced twenty minutes a day, are likely to prove survival beyond death. Many have used them as a direct route to Self-Realization, where one learns his mission in life. The next stage, God Consciousness, is the joyful state wherein Soul becomes the spiritual traveler, an agent for God. The underlying principle one learns is this: Soul exists because God loves It.

Study of ECKANKAR includes:

1. Twelve monthly lessons of *The ECK Dream Discourses,* which include these titles: "Dreams—The Bridge to Heaven," "The Dream Master," "How to Interpret Your Dreams," "Dream Travel to Soul Travel," and more. You may study them alone at home or in a class with others.

2. The *Mystic World,* a quarterly newsletter with a Wisdom Note and articles by the Living ECK Master. In it are also letters and articles from students of Eckankar around the world.

3. Special mailings to keep you informed of upcoming Eckankar seminars and activities around the world, new study materials available from Eckankar, and more.

4. The opportunity to attend ECK Satsang classes and book discussions with others in your community.

5. Initiation eligibility.

6. Attendance at certain chela meetings at ECK seminars.

How to Find Out More:

Call **(612) 544-0066**, Monday through Friday, 8 a.m. to 5 p.m. central time, to find out more about how to study *The ECK Dream Discourses,* or use the coupon at the back of this book. Or write: **ECKANKAR, Att: ECK Study, P.O. Box 27300, Minneapolis, MN 55427 U.S.A.**

Introductory Books on ECKANKAR

 The Book of ECK Parables, Volume One, Harold Klemp

Learn how to find spiritual fulfillment in everyday life from this series of over ninety light, easy-reading stories by Eckankar's spiritual leader, Sri Harold Klemp. The parables reveal secrets of Soul Travel, dreams, karma, health, reincarnation, and—most important of all—initiation into the Sound and Light of God, in everyday settings we can understand.

 ECKANKAR—The Key to Secret Worlds, Paul Twitchell

Paul Twitchell, modern-day founder of Eckankar, gives you the basics of this ancient teaching. Includes six specific Soul Travel exercises to see the Light and hear the Sound of God, plus case histories of Soul Travel. Learn to recognize yourself as Soul—and journey into the heavens of the Far Country.

 The Wind of Change, Harold Klemp

What are the hidden spiritual reasons behind every event in your life? With stories drawn from his own lifelong training, Eckankar's spiritual leader shows you how to use the power of Spirit to discover those reasons. Follow him from the Wisconsin farm of his youth, to a military base in Japan; from a job in Texas, into the realms beyond, as he shares the secrets of Eckankar.

 The Tiger's Fang, Paul Twitchell

Paul Twitchell's teacher, Rebazar Tarzs, takes him on a journey through vast worlds of Light and Sound, to sit at the feet of the spiritual Masters. Their conversations bring out the secret of how to draw closer to God—and awaken Soul to Its spiritual destiny. Many have used this book, with its vivid descriptions of heavenly worlds and citizens, to begin their own spiritual adventures.

For more information about the books and teachings of Eckankar, please write: **ECKANKAR, Att: Information, P.O. Box 27300, Minneapolis, MN 55427 U.S.A.**

Or look under **ECKANKAR** in your local phone book for an Eckankar Center near you.

There May Be an
ECKANKAR Study Group near You

Eckankar offers a variety of local and international activities for the spiritual seeker. With hundreds of study groups worldwide, Eckankar is near you! Many areas have Eckankar Centers where you can browse through the books in a quiet, unpressured environment, talk with others who share an interest in this ancient teaching, and attend beginning discussion classes on how to gain the attributes of Soul: wisdom, power, love, and freedom.

Around the world, Eckankar study groups offer special one-day or weekend seminars on the basic teachings of Eckankar. Check your phone book under **ECKANKAR**, or call **(612) 544-0066** for membership information and the location of the Eckankar Center or study group nearest you. Or write **ECKANKAR, Att: Information, P.O. Box 27300, Minneapolis, MN 55427 U.S.A.**

☐ Please send me information on the nearest Eckankar discussion or study group in my area.

☐ I would like an application form to study Eckankar further. Please send me more information about the twelve-month Eckankar study discourses on dreams.

Please type or print clearly   941

Name _____

Street _____ Apt. # ____

City _____ State/Prov. _____

Zip/Postal Code _____ Country _____

(Our policy: Your name and address are held in strict confidence. We do not rent or sell our mailing lists. Nor will anyone call on you. Our purpose is only to show people the ECK way home to God.)

Eckankar, Att: Information, P.O. Box 27300, Minneapolis, MN 55427, U.S.A.